13TH AGE

SHADOWS OF ELDOLAN

A *13TH AGE* ADVENTURE FOR 1ST-LEVEL HEROES

BY **CAL MOORE**

Pelgrane Press

13TH AGE IS A FANTASY ROLEPLAYING GAME BY
**ROB HEINSOO, JONATHAN TWEET,
LEE MOYER, & AARON MCCONNELL**

FIRE OPAL

www.fireopalmedia.com and www.pelgranepress.com

CREDITS

PUBLISHER
Simon Rogers

ASSISTANT PUBLISHER
Cathriona Tobin

AUTHOR
Cal Moore

ART DIRECTION
Cal Moore
Cathriona Tobin

ARTWORK
Joshua Calloway

CARTOGRAPHY
Pär Lindström

LAYOUT
Chris Huth

ADDITIONAL DEVELOPMENT AND DESIGN
Rob Heinsoo

EDITING
Cal Moore

PLAYTESTERS

Kendall Jung, Derek Dokter, Tim Gray, Matt Riley, Leland Zavadil, Paul Venner, Chris Petty, Steve Holt, Neil Williams, Matt Clarke, Nikodemus Siivola, Antti Kanner, Hanna Järvinen, Katri Lassila, Mika Koverola, Toni Sihvonen, Eran Aviram, Aviv Or, Evyatar Amitay, Assaf Hershko, Hadas Elber-Aviram, Timothy Baker, Christopher Fransioli, Chelsea Johnson, Rhiannon Pullin, Joe Stroup, Mitchell, Robby, Alex, Doug Jacobson, Joe Smith, Marc Weddle, Steve Robinson, Rich Williams

Special thanks to Rob Heinsoo for his insights in helping me turn the dial on this adventure to 13.

TABLE OF

CONTENTS

INTRODUCTION

Shadows of Eldolan is an introductory adventure for the *13th Age* game system. The adventure's objective is to provide a GM with a fun and interesting plot with easy-to-run battles that will challenge the players, while providing strong story elements that fit with the design concepts and use of icons in the *13th Age* system. The adventure also gives the GM a town setting near the Archmage's city of Horizon in the Dragon Empire to use as a source of adventure and intrigue for the PCs.

Compared to some of the wilder *13th Age* adventures, *Shadows of Eldolan* plays it straight. Your campaign will already be loaded with plot hooks and complications thanks to the PCs' *uniques* and backgrounds. Weirdness may be just around the corner, but it can be the PCs who supply it, if that's how they're oriented. Therefore we've presented Eldolan as a straightforward mix of business districts, NPCs just trying to keep their heads above water, and duelling wizards' schools. There's ample room for your campaign's *unique* embroidery, if that's how you're oriented.

Of course, the story elements and locale can easily fit into any d20 system game, and a GM can replace the statistical elements with those that fit the system they're running. Enjoy!

ADVENTURE OVERVIEW

Here's the story so far and the setup for the adventure. We'll follow this summary with notes on running adventures in Eldolan, then get into the full flow of the statted-out adventure on page 12.

FOLLOWING A DARK PATH

The story revolves around a servant of the Lich King, and the adventure mostly features enemies linked to that icon. As always, you should weave each PC's one unique thing and current icon relationships into the story where it feels right. Other icons could be secretly aiding the Lich King's servants, or perhaps acting to thwart anyone trying to hinder his servant's plans (and thus hinder the One-eyed Lord), because it suits that icon's purposes for whatever reason.

For this story, the PCs' links to the Lich King mostly come from their interaction with a wizard in his service, Garados Kessmir, who has delved into dark secrets of undeath and magic and seeks knowledge that only the Lich King can grant. Garados is a wizard in Eldolan, a port town along Pocket Bay about 20 miles northeast of Horizon. Like many with magical talent in the region, Garados is also a noble. In addition, his family controls the profitable Lamplighter's Guild in Eldolan, and he holds both wealth and power thanks to that association.

When Garados was a young apprentice at the Mithril wizard school, he discovered the diary of a wizard named Tarloc who had lived 200 years earlier. Tarloc had researched "dark topics" that were banned by the instructors at the school. Intrigued, Garados learned how the Wizard King of old had been a more powerful spellcaster than even the Archmage, and that much knowledge now called "dark arts" by the Archmage's people had been hidden away in ancient sites by the Wizard King (the current Lich King) during his reign. It also included a ritual to summon a familiar with a connection to the Lich King. Wanting the lost knowledge, Garados performed the ritual and summoned his familiar Kos, a homunculus that looks like a skeletal monkey, and thus began his path down the road to darkness.

It has been over twenty-five years since Garados discovered the diary, and he is now the head of his family and leader of the Lamplighter's Guild, an organization that owns the contract for keeping the magical lamps of Eldolan lit after sunset. In addition to those responsibilities, Garados runs a curiosity shop in the Grounds with an old classmate, Laredes the Sage, who has no idea of Garados' secret life. Over the years, Garados has been acquiring power and learning the secrets the Lich King is willing to share through Kos.

THE PRICE OF LOYALTY

Most recently, Garados has been working on a special project through knowledge gained from his master via Kos and from a book of dark magic rituals that came into the store. He has nearly assembled a formula for animating once-dead flesh to create powerful and difficult-to-harm constructs fueled by necrotic energy. But the Lich King's necromancers have refused to give Garados the final part of the ritual unless he's willing to show his loyalty to his master publicly (and also as a reminder to the wizard of the ties that bind him). To do so, the Lich King's lieutenants have ordered Garados to unleash the undead he and his people have been creating upon the town "to remind them that death always waits for them" and also to send a few more souls into the darkness.

A character with a positive relationship with the Lich King won't *necessarily* be inclined to help Garados achieve his goal (and won't be aware of his activities initially anyway). Competition among the One-eyed Lord's servants is fierce; perhaps the PC seeks to gain the knowledge that Garados has acquired, the Lich King's people are unhappy that the execution of the attack in the square was less than satisfactory (the "pumpkin incident,") or some other factor will motivate a player to want to put an end to the Seekers of the Lost (or to achieve another outcome). There could be factions among the Lich King's followers that would pit the PCs against whoever is pulling Garados' strings. Talk to such players away from the group once the truth of the Lich King's involvement through Garados and the Seekers becomes obvious and figure out a way to make it work for the story.

Garados was not fully prepared for this request since he was focused on obtaining a position on Eldolan's Mage Council, but wanting the final piece of the ritual (and not wanting to anger his master), he has spent the last few weeks arranging a proper show for the Lich King with the help of the Seekers of the Lost—a cult of Lich King followers that he has assembled and installed within Eldolan and the Lamplighter's Guild over the last ten years.

To honor his master's command, Garados has planned a very public attack in one of Eldolan's main squares against the town guard and a rival icon to show the populace that just because they live behind high walls with magic wards, death can still touch them at any time. The attack also serves a secondary purpose, since it will provide Garados with more fresh bodies to put to good use on his project once he pleases the Lich King and gains the last part of the ritual he seeks. And so, Garados has set in motion a . . .

ZOMBIE ATTACK!

The action starts when Garados and his people release a group of zombies upon the populace in Hawker's Square, though Garados's servants slightly spoil the "horrifying" spectacle he had hoped for by placing one of their zombies in a cart full of pumpkins. The undead attack the townsfolk in the square, targeting the Silver Shields—Eldolan's town watch—and also a representative of an icon that the PCs are meeting there, drawing the adventurers into the conflict. After the heroes fight off the zombies, town officials and mages swoop in to discover what happened.

The watchmen of the Silver Shields, realizing that their members were targeted and already dealing with other problems in town, will be unwilling to provide any help as they pull back to secure their defenses and watch for further attacks. They are not prepared to face such a threat, since their primary duties involve maintaining order in the town and cleaning up messes made by the wizards at the schools of magic.

Seeing that the Shields will be of little use, and realizing that political intrigues and school rivalries among the ruling wizards will hamper any investigation, the icon's representative enlists the PCs (one way or another) to discover who was behind the attack and why that icon's power is being challenged, as well as to put an end to the threat if possible.

FOLLOWING THE CLUES

As the heroes travel the districts of Eldolan seeking those responsible for the attack, they will encounter NPCs with information they need and have to battle the Seekers of the Lost and their allies, as well as others who wish to see the heroes fail, or those who are more bold now that the Shields aren't around. One lead will take the PCs slightly off course, into the waiting arms of a group of Diabolist cultists near the Docks. Another will take them to the city's crypts, the Dead Vaults, in the Temple district where they will face a Seeker priest who works for Garados . . . and the undead servants he has been secretly creating. Yet another lead takes the PCs to an old dwarven brewery in the Saddle where some Seeker agents are holed up. A different lead will take them to the Commons, where a servant of the Priestess running a poor house sets them upon the path of the Dreammaster, a man who has recently set up his new business and who has a connection to the Seekers. Other leads not outlined in this adventure can be fleshed out by the GM as needed.

The heroes' investigation will lead them to Seekers of the Lost agents, and eventually to the Lamplighter's Guild's main office in the Saddle, a place called the Lanternwerks. Initial investigations may provide little real information, since the Seekers are well hidden within the guild. The PCs might also learn of the Lamplighter's Guild's leader, Garados, who has a curiosity shop in the Grounds. An initial encounter with Garados will put him on the defensive, but the PCs should have little evidence of his involvement initially as he falsely promises to help root out any evil that could be in his organization. Knowing that the heroes could delay or ruin the Seekers' plans, Garados or one of his servants will arrange an ambush, using both living and undead servants to discourage the PCs' investigation.

Eventually the group will learn of a Seeker leader within the Lanternwerks, Arlissa Thent. They will have to confront and defeat her and her Seeker allies. Once they do, a critical letter reveals that Arlissa isn't the Seeker's leader—the attack was orchestrated by Garados.

As evidence against Garados and the Seekers of the Lost mounts, a return trip to the curiosity shop reveals that Garados is gone, but his business partner Laredes is there. If the PCs deal well with the wizard, Laredes will reveal Garados' hidden lair.

THE FINAL SHOWDOWN

Through Laredes' help, the heroes' icon connections, interrogating members of the Seekers cult, and/or other investigation, the PCs will eventually discover Garados' private sanctum, a lair with tunnel connections to the curiosity shop in the Grounds, the Dead Vaults in the Temple district, and a small square near the mission in the Commons. The PCs will have to fight through traps and guardians to reach the hidden sanctum, where Garados and his allies wait, including his greatest creation, a flesh golem that is almost completed.

TIMELINE OF EVENTS BEFORE THE ATTACK

Here's a timeline to help GMs have a better understanding of what events lead up to the attack, giving a big-picture view for the larger story and how the Seekers are involved.

- Garados finds Tarloc's diary, completes a summoning ritual for his familiar Kos, and becomes dedicated to the Lich King.
- Garados creates the Seekers of the Lost and gains control of the Lamplighter's Guild from his family.
- Garados' agents begin to instill themselves into organizations and positions all over the city, especially the Lamplighter's Guild.
- Garados finds a book of dark rituals that will allow him to create a flesh golem and begins collecting bodies. The Lich King's lieutenants require a display of obedience to gain the last piece of the ritual. Garados instructs Arlissa Thent on the plan, and she relays all of his orders.
- Needing suitable bodies for the zombie attack, Garados instructs Aerto to step up his efforts. He also tells Paulos and Sigmund to be more aggressive in taking street folk from the Commons.
- Garados tells Landon to prepare some zombies from the crypts for the attack. Landon sends them to the lab through a secret tunnel from the Dead Vaults.
- Grayson and Jalen acquire a cart from Pazarias Rane two days before the attack and stash it at the old brewery.

WHAT KIND OF ADVENTURE IS THIS?

While many *13th Age* adventures will be full of exotic locations and big magic events that fall under the "high fantasy" heading, this adventure tones things down slightly. There are still plenty of magical events, situations, and opponents, but the PCs are starting their careers in a town location, and they will face enemies that are more in-line with what you might expect for starting heroes in that setting . . . though ones touched by the Lich King's influence in many cases. Feel free to ratchet up the high fantasy elements to suit your needs if that's what your group prefers.

As for the enemies the PCs will face, each scene only uses one set of stat blocks rather than multiple options based on icon relationships. But the GM should feel free to reflavor (or change) those enemies to fit the PCs and their relationships. In an effort to save space, we're letting each GM make that adjustment as needed rather than providing multiple options.

As far as locations go, the adventure provides one view of what Eldolan is like. But it doesn't have to be that way. The GM should feel free to change things up, or to ask the players to describe locations/districts and change the game to fit that view. Just remember to be consistent with such descriptions on future visits.

- The night before the attack, Sigmund and Paulos walk the zombies at the lab to the edge of the square; the zombies are disguised with hooded robes. The Seekers stash the zombies inside the overflow chamber, helped by Seeker Lamplighters under Arlissa's orders who keep the square dark until it's done.
- The day of the attack, Sigmund and Paulos bring five more zombies to the square's northeast entrance, again disguised by robes. As a trigger to the attack, they release the zombies as the Silver Shields in the square draw near.
- The day of the attack, Grayson and Jalen drive the cart to the square. It's filled with pumpkins and holds an additional zombie. To have some fun, Jalen puts a pumpkin head on it. They set the cart in place, and tip it back when the first screams start. Grayson casts the zombie targeting spell upon the PCs' contact as both men flee the square.
- The zombies attack!

ADVENTURING IN ELDOLAN

As the PCs gain clues about the attack, they may visit and learn about nearly every district of the town of Eldolan. Each area has a basic description that you can flesh out as much as you like. Eldolan could even be a "home base" for the PCs as they become mighty heroes.

Eldolan is close enough to the city of Horizon to have strong connections with the Archmage's network of wizards and arcane institutions, so magic is a common element within the town. But the other icons also have a presence there, to a lesser or greater extent as fits the PCs. The town can have whatever feel you wish it to have, but magic should generally be a part of everyday life for the townsfolk.

Here are a few options you can seed throughout the adventure to give the town a greater magical feel:

- Lamplighter's Guild wizards lighting lanterns around town at dusk.
- Warded buildings with strange architecture connected to the Archmage's weather control system.
- City gates, district walls, houses, and other areas guarded by magical wards.
- Street magic performances (magic fireworks, shadow puppets, etc.).
- Occasional magical shadows cast by great lights blooming among the airborne towers of Horizon.
- Magical sprites zipping through the air, delivering messages around the city.

GEOGRAPHY AND TOWN LAYOUT

Eldolan lies 20 miles northeast of Horizon and is built upon the shores of Pocket Bay between two ridges that look like the high edges of a saddle. The low, smooth ends open to the north and to the south. The north end contains the port and is known simply as "the Docks." The south end holds two districts: the small Temple district along the eastern edge of the town, where people can consult the gods and their priests and attend the town crypts—the Dead Vaults; and the much larger Commons to the west, where simple craftsfolk and laborers work and live.

Built into the high ridge to the east a few hundred feet above sea level are the buildings of the Schools of Magic (called the Grounds). The buildings in the district look down the slope upon the rest of the town, with a high wall separating it from the other districts. On the back side of the Grounds, high cliffs fall to the sea and coastline. Upon the western ridge, and slightly lower in elevation than the Grounds to the east, are the buildings and structures of the Mage Council and other government buildings (the Governs). The middle part of the town, which locals call

"the Saddle," houses the higher-end merchant shops and other industry.

A small river called Uller's Flow enters the town under the walls in the Commons, passes underground through the Saddle, and emerges again in the Docks, where it empties into the sea helping form the bay.

Each district is outlined in a relevant section in the adventure. The only one that doesn't have a direct lead connected to it (unless you choose to send the PCs there) is the Governs, so its description is presented here.

THE GOVERNS

Sitting high on the western edge of Eldolan overlooking the sea to the west and the Saddle to the east, the Governs is where the business of ruling Eldolan occurs. The district is smaller than the Grounds opposite it, but the single gate through the interior district wall is no less well-guarded. Only those who rule the city—nobles and wizards and bureaucrats—visit the district, or perhaps the occasional important town merchant seeking some ruling or advantage. It's also the site of the town courts, with high-profile prisoners imprisoned in the small dungeon below the district (lesser criminals go to Silver Shield jails in the Commons). The Archmage's people are everywhere in the Governs, and there's also an Imperial outpost there for the Empire-appointed mayor (Alanis Arvanette), though she has little power compared to the Mage Council. There are many wards upon the government buildings, and plenty of guards, both mundane and magical, to keep most mischief out. Unless a character's unique suggests it, or a PC uses an advantage from their connection with an icon (or they're willing to bribe heavily), the PCs will have a tough time getting into the district (DC 20 skill checks).

RULERSHIP AND LAW

Like Horizon, magic and magical talent defines who you are in Eldolan. Most nobles are also wizards, and quite a few of the town's craftsfolk have some amount of arcane skill. The town is ruled by a Mage Council of five wizards who are politically connected (Garados is in the running for the next council seat to open). They make all major decisions for the town and have strong connections to the Archmage. Unfortunately, they and the bureaucracy that serves them rarely seem to get much done due to the petty bickering, provincial disputes, and school rivalries that pit them against each other more often than it has them solving town issues. The constant cronyism and playing favorites that goes on among the Council members and their servants ensures that stagnation and the status quo is the common state

ELDOLAN

POCKET BAY

0.1 0.2 0.3 0.4 0.5 miles

DOCKS SCHOO
GOVERNS
GROUN
SADDLE
TEMPL
COMMONS
WARRENS

of things in town. Those who want action in Eldolan usually have to find ways of solving issues themselves.

Imperial law is practiced in Eldolan (whatever that means in your game), but less enforced outside the Saddle, Governs, Temples, and Grounds due to the limits of the Silver Shields. Considerations are often made for magical mishaps and similar issues that would normally break the law in other places. Allied or hired wizards may duel over issues that no one wants to go to the courts or to the Council. Some of those duels result in death, and even occasionally the deaths of both duelists, when neither party bothers with defense.

With the watchmen of the Silver Shields skittish, Eldolan is more dangerous than normal. The Shields will have more and larger patrols in the markets and more affluent districts of town during the day, but will have limited patrols in the poorer districts and during the night (pulling them completely from the Docks and Commons during the dark hours).

If the PCs find themselves in a situation that pits them against the Silver Shields for some reason, stats for a Silver Shield sergeant and watchers are at the back of the adventure in the NPC Stats section (see page 66).

THE SCHOOLS OF MAGIC

One difficulty that the Eldolan populace has to deal with, and something that may interfere with the PCs' investigation, is the fact that the town houses three distinct Schools of Magic in the Grounds. Each school has a different take on magic and how it's best practiced, and they tend to view the others unfavorably. This creates rivalries between the groups, which often manifest in the form of magical pranks or outright confrontations between the members of the different schools. The wizards usually resolve these issues among themselves, but often the Silver Shields or other town leaders need to be called in to adjudicate, especially when property damage occurs.

Even though each School of Magic is a separate group, they all share the classrooms, study halls, libraries, and other structures of the Grounds, though each group provides its own instructors. The head instructor of each School reports to the Headmaster, a wizard who is supposed to be objective in all rulings, but rarely is fully, since that wizard comes from one of the three schools (currently a human Eldritch Master named **Tobias Longshadow**).

The wizards of each school are required to wear school robes while enrolled, though the colors and designs vary. Instructors also wear the same style of robes, though with more ornamentation, and many of those who graduate continue the practice afterward, making "wizard robes" a very common item of clothing in the town (and making it difficult to identify anyone wearing such robes without more details because stealing a rival group's robes to impersonate them is a well-known tactic).

The three Schools of Magic include:

THE ELDRITCH MASTERS

Consisting mostly of high elves and half elves but with a few human casters in the ranks too, the Eldritch Masters focus on perfecting big rituals and flashy spells that make a lot of noise and deal a lot of damage. They wear blue robes with silver stitching showing arcane runes, and their crest is a silver lightning bolt. **Sharissa Darkbolt**, a high elf wizard, is the lead instructor of the school.

MITHRIL

This group's ranks mostly contain human wizards, though a few half-elves and dwarves with some artificing talent are found among them. They focus on crafting magical implements, potions, oils, runes, and other items that can hold magic, and they rely on magical equipment more than the other groups. They wear robes of dark silver with golden stitching showing runes and diagrams of machines. Their symbol is a mithril gear. **Cornigar Ulson**, a human wizard of ancient years, is the lead instructor of the school.

ARCANISTS OF THE HIDDEN VEIL

The members of this school are mixed, including gnomes, halflings, elves (mostly drow), humans, and a few others. They practice the magic of stealth and misdirection, with illusion and trickery being the focus, as well as rituals that are powerful but subtle. Some claim that they seek a different reality, one that is hidden by a veil of magic that only a few know how to pierce. They wear gray robes the color of spidersilk, with black stitching. Their symbol is a closed eye. **Jarlin the Sly**, a gnome wizard and illusionist, is the lead instructor of the school.

STEPPING INTO A MAGICAL SHOWDOWN

If at any point you're in need of a random event or battle to grab the players' attention, consider dropping them into the middle of a magical showdown between wizards of two (or three) Schools, aka Big-Trouble-in-Little-China style. The lack of a Silver Shield presence might have brought out some old grudges.

The PCs emerge into an alley or walk into a square to see wizards of the rival Schools facing off. It could be a situation where the PCs have a chance of convincing the wizards to go their separate ways if that's something the players would respond to. Or it could be that they enter the middleground just as the first magic bolt is launched and they have to escape the area or fight off wizards from one school or another who think they are with their rivals. Stats for students and an instructor from each school are in the NPC Stats section on page 66.

Of course, if the PCs help one side over another, they will instantly make friends and enemies of those groups, with consequences of your choosing throughout the adventure.

POPULACE

Eldolan's population is mixed, though humans are the majority. The Schools of Magic draw wizards from many other races, however, and high elves are the most common of those. Being a port town, plenty of halfling sailors and scoundrels are active in the Docks, as is a small contingent of dwarven dockworkers who carry goods from the ships. Half-elves can be found in smaller numbers running the many taverns and inns throughout the town, or working in them as musicians. Half-orcs are more scarce, except as bodyguards to nobles and merchants. Other races can be found in smaller numbers throughout the town.

GOODS AND SERVICES

Being a town of wizards, and not far from Horizon, all sort of strange goods come through Eldolan. The PCs can find magical components and simple magical crafts of all types in the Saddle and Grounds. As a port town, most types of normal goods also enter the town from other ports on the Midland Sea. With the Schools of Magic in the town, merchants and travelers are always arriving with rare antiquities, items rare and wondrous, and artifacts of the most powerful type—some of which might actually be as claimed. The Prince's folk also run a thriving black market for those goods that the Council of Mages might frown upon but don't attempt to disrupt. If a PC can't find something in Eldolan, it can surely be brought in from Horizon, for the right price.

If the PCs wish to purchase items while in town, the various shops and craftsfolk carry all items listed in the core book rules. In addition, they can also purchase the following special items with minor enchantments (mostly from graduated Mithril artificers in the Saddle). Feel free to expand on such items, though none should provide the PCs with a large direct benefit.

Item	Price (gp)
Bug bomb (drives out vermin)	2 gp
Expandable container (holds as much as 4 containers of same size)	30–500 gp
Festival lights (floating candles that lose magic when burnt out)	5 gp each
Hexward (iron item hung by silver nails that keeps fey and spirits away)	20 gp
Lodestone compass (points out north, or east, or whatever it's attuned to)	25 gp
Bright-burning (hot) lantern oil, 1 pint	4 gp
Magical fireworks: sky blasts, snap-pops, smoke monsters, screamers	5 gp each

OTHER PROBLEMS IN ELDOLAN

While the zombie attack is about to be the most pressing (and public) issue the town faces, it's not a static place and there are other problems waiting to be revealed. If it makes sense for the PCs' story, feel free to include one or more of the following possibilities to the mix. Be careful about adding too many side-plots, however; one or two, particularly for sessions when some of the players are absent, could help keep the pressure on, making it clear that the Silver Shields have many issues to deal with that are stretching them thin. Conversely, if your PCs slam through the investigation too easily, these subplots can slow them down to buy you time to figure out how you want to handle the main plot with the Seekers. See the NPC Stats section at the back of the adventure (page 66) for stat blocks related to the three possible subplots mentioned below.

- A recent poorly performed experiment by one of the Eldritch Masters set an ochre jelly free in the town sewers. The school members are trying to fix the problem discreetly but haven't been able to find the creature so far. On the plus side the sewers are empty of rats. On the minus side, the streets are full of rats. *(page 68)*
- Diabolist cultists in the Docks district have recently summoned an imp and let it free to cause trouble in the area. It's manipulating a ship captain and her crew into causing trouble. At your option, GM, the Shields could be too thin to help because their efforts are being focused on capturing the imp. *(page 69)*
- Rumors of a large camp of demonic gnoll raiders near Gorogan's Maw to the east have brought many strike-groups dedicated to the Crusader and paladins dedicated to the Great Gold Worm into the area. There's been a lot of friction between the groups. They might end up providing surprising help to the PCs (via an icon relationship roll or two) or they might get the PCs embroiled in a "Who's the True Defender" turf skirmish. *(page 69)*

WORKING IN THE ICONS

Lots of people in Eldolan have no iconic connections. But plenty more are connected to the icons, and to the Archmage in particular considering the town's location. The Emperor, the Priestess, and the Prince all hold sway over various elements of the town as well. Other icons might have less obvious connections in the town, but are all workable into the storyline.

When the PCs use an ability or effect that makes an icon connection, feel free to adjust the current storyline to fit the new connection. Perhaps the bard made a Balladeer roll for the Prince of Shadows but then rolled a 5 on his relationship dice, so now the gang of street toughs the heroes are facing were hired by a representative of the Three to slow the party down and thwart the Prince, or maybe the gang's leader is trying to retrieve an item from the PCs that was stolen from the Prince's people. Make sure the stories are relevant to the PCs!

The adventure includes suggestions where it makes sense to let the players make icon rolls to their advantage, including rolls to set the adventure in motion after the zombie attack. It also has "Icon Involvements" sidebars that suggest storylines that the PCs might encounter while in different districts. The GM should also feel free to use any of the strategies outlined in the core rules for icon interactions, especially rolling at the start of each session, and letting those rolls suggest interactions that might happen during that leg of the adventure.

DEFAULT ASSUMPTIONS ABOUT THE HEROES

The battles outlined in this adventure assume a party of 5 PCs. Each battle will list adjustments for the GM to make if there are only 4 PCs or if there are 6 PCs. Adjustments beyond that are up to the GM using the *13th Age* core rules. Adjustments aren't made to the loot rewards in the adventure for different numbers of PCs, however. Manage those totals as you see fit.

The adventure doesn't specify full heal-up break points since the PCs could follow any of the leads, or others you create if you're using the core rules, that suggest one full heal-up every four battles. We would suggest, however, that you try not to give the PCs a full heal-up right before the final battle of each lead unless the PCs are seriously underpowered going into it. Then reward them with a full heal-up after the big fight. They should definitely have a few daily powers/spells and recoveries left before facing Garados at the end of the adventure.

If you're using the incremental advance rules and allowing the PCs to increase their capabilities between sessions, you also might want to increase the difficulty of battles later in the adventure. Add a few extra mooks or perhaps an additional non-named opponent to the fight. Each of the battles in the leads is balanced toward a starting group of 1st level characters, whether the battle is normal or double-strength.

THE STORY BEGINS

[Don't have the PCs roll icon relationship dice at the start of the session; wait until after the zombie fight below. Later, groups can roll relationship dice at the start of each session per the core book rules.]

Before starting the adventure, choose one heroic or ambiguous icon to which the majority of the PCs have a connection. The heroes have recently arrived in Eldolan to meet with a representative of that icon for various reasons. Have each player describe the circumstances that brought their character to Eldolan in regards to that icon, even if they don't have a personal relationship with the icon. You can link these story connections to the adventures the PCs have in town, and also have the icon's representative use them as leverage to enlist the heroes' help.

Currently, the PCs are in Hawker's Square, the main square in the Commons district not far from the main gates, and it's filled with people shopping and moving through to other locations in town. There are a few semi-permanent booths and tents set up in the middle and around the edges of the square selling all manner of goods and foods. Many individuals are peddling their wares on blankets or tables along the thoroughfares. If it makes sense for the icon in play, the PCs' contact can have a cover identity as a buyer for a noble house. The PCs are approaching the contact's location when the action starts.

The icon you choose determines which NPC the characters will be interacting with. Each contact has a bit of personal information attached—use the personality notes judiciously if your PCs are the type to seize on any oddity as a red herring:

- **Archmage:** Jadu, a magical sprite. It's sentient and has been forced to continue service to the Archmage even though it was promised its freedom.
- **Crusader:** Marstad Trueson, male human. He bears a magical silver hand in place of the one he lost fighting demons in a hellhole raid, but its magic is fading.
- **Dwarf King:** Voln son of Koln, male dwarf. He seeks to raise the standing of his clan, the Stoneraiders, while also taking care of the King's business.
- **Elf Queen:** Mirias Goldeneyes, female high elf. Her family was murdered by raiders flying the Orc Lord's banners and she looks for opportunities to set the heroes upon that enemy.
- **Emperor:** Raley Tallfellow, male halfling. Some at the capital claim that Raley has had dealings with the Prince of Shadows as part of his services to the Empire.
- **Great Gold Wyrm:** Therilsa Stormhand, female half elf. She comes from a line of half-elves who maintain some of the Archmage's devices controlling the weather in the Empire.
- **High Druid:** Korvas Graymane, male half-orc. He was banished from his clan for an unspeakable offense.
- **Priestess:** Camilla, daughter of the Light, female human. She is a DEVOUT follower.
- **Prince of Shadows:** Zoristar Twoscars, male dark elf. Rumors suggest his father is brokering a deal between the Prince and the Elf Queen.

OR USE A PC AS THE CONTACT!

If you're introducing a new character to the game, or you want to ratchet up the tension and roleplaying, have one of the PCs be the contact (and be targeted by the zombies). Some players love that type of thing.

Read the following to the players (and don't worry, this is the longest read-aloud text in the adventure! If you're an experienced GM who hates descriptive text blocks and think they should have died out in the 90s, feel free to ignore them and describe things as you wish, but be sure to set the stage well to aid the gridless system): *As the afternoon wanes, the shadows of the three-story, gray stone buildings that form the perimeter of Hawker's Square are lengthening, and the calls of vendors and beggars alike are growing louder. Suddenly, a loud crash rises above the babel of voices. On the western side of the square a large wagon full of pumpkins has tipped backward, filling the roadway with tumbling gourds. At first people laugh. Then a woman's scream cuts through the air.*

As the crowd parts, you see someone is fighting with a Silver Shield town watcher near one of the square's two unblocked exits to the northeast, and a woman next to them is screaming and pointing. You understand her wails as the other combatant lunges forward to bite the guard's throat and pulls back with blood-stained jaws. Then more yells erupt as you see a group of figures emerge from a stairwell in the center of the square and quickly overwhelm the last two Silver Shield guards in the area. The figures are humanoid . . . and were once living. Now, you see that they surely are not, because each one has large, open wounds where entrails, or lung, or heart, or eye are missing.

Suddenly, you hear a crackling sound behind you and turn to see your surprised-looking contact being surrounded in a magical whirlwind of dark shadows and purple vapors. As one, the group of zombies turns toward [contact's name here] and begins to advance, driving the doomed townsfolk before them to the ground as the rest of the crowd screams and fearfully rushes toward the last remaining exit to the southwest. The rush is stopped by a roaring zombie wearing a pumpkin with a leering face carved into it. Only you stand in the creatures' way.

As the area clears, the PCs see that one of the square's three exits is blocked by the tipped pumpkin cart, another is blocked by five rotting figures—zombies!—standing in a group across the entrance, and the last is plugged by the mass of people fleeing the square, leaving no easy escape. The main group of zombies emerges from the stairwell in the center of the square. (See map on page 14). **Roll initiative!**

Tactics: The undead creatures blocking the northeast exit (including the one that bit the guard) are a mob of **five zombie shufflers**. Those five won't attack the PCs unless they are attacked; their purpose is to block the exit, though one begins to eat at the now dead town guard. Spreading out in a wedge shape from the stairwell is separate mob of **ten zombie shufflers**, as well as **two putrefying human zombies** (at the back of the wedge). The PCs' contact has been targeted with a spell to draw the undead, but the zombies will also attack anyone who moves near them or attacks them. The figure by the cart is a **zombie pumpkin hurler**, whose appearance would be humorous if it weren't so deadly with its ammunition.

Have the heroes start the battle slightly spread out from each other in the square as indicated on the map overleaf but still nearby each other (if you're using a game map/terrain, have each player indicate their PC's starting position in the center or southern end of the square when their first turn starts). There is some minor cover in the form of tents and tables in the area, and any dicey actions a PC wants to make to use the terrain to their advantage requires a DC 15 check to succeed. Make it clear to the PCs which zombies are mooks (their removed organs have caused heavy damage to the body) and which are the more intact putrefying human zombies, unless you want to make the battle more difficult for the PCs. The mooks will intercept PCs trying to move toward the putrefying human zombies, however.

The NPC contact starts the battle far away from all of the zombies at the southern end of the square and goes last in round. The contact will use move actions to escape/avoid the zombies instead of fighting (+5 to disengage) and will try to move behind a PC who can intercept the zombies. If the battle is going badly for the PCs, you could have a zombie or two waste an attack on the contact, but the goal is for the zombies to face the PCs and for the contact to survive.

This battle is tougher than average (but not quite double) to set the tone for the adventure. If there are only 4 PCs, remove one putrefying human zombie. If there are 6 PCs, add another putrefying human zombie and 2 zombie shufflers to the mob of 10 at the center of the square.

ZOMBIE SHUFFLERS

"Mwauurgh . . ."

1st level mook [UNDEAD]
Initiative: +0
Vulnerability: holy

Rotting fist +5 vs. AC—3 damage
   Natural 16+: Both the zombie and its target take 1d4 damage!

Headshot: A critical hit against a zombie shuffler deals triple damage instead of the normal double damage for a crit.

AC	14	
PD	12	**HP 10 (mook)**
MD	8	

Mook: Kill one zombie shuffler mook for every 10 damage you deal to the mob.

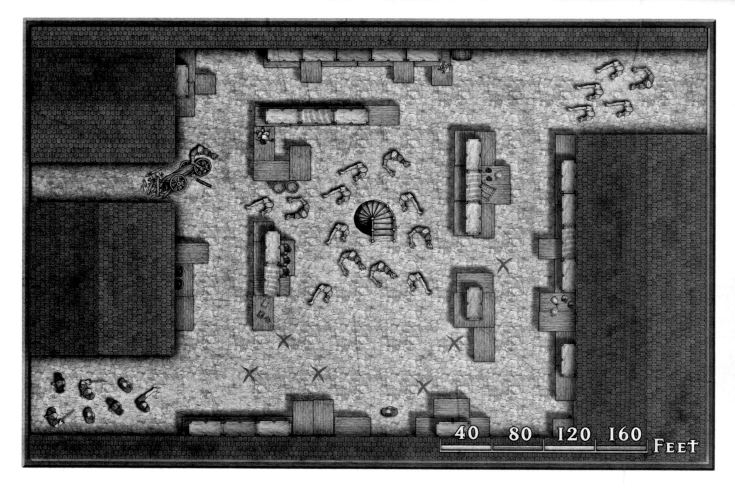

PUTREFYING HUMAN ZOMBIES

"Scrape . . .scrape . . . smash."

2nd level troop [UNDEAD]
Initiative: +1
Vulnerability: holy

Rotting fist +7 vs. AC—6 damage
   Natural 16+: Both the zombie and its target take 1d6 damage!

Headshot: A critical hit against a zombie drops it to 0 hp.

Open putrefying wounds: When a living, non-construct creature
   starts its turn engaged with the zombie, it must roll an easy
   save (6+). On a failure, it takes a −2 penalty to attacks and
   damage with melee attacks against the zombie that turn.

AC	15	
PD	13	**HP 60**
MD	9	

ZOMBIE PUMPKIN HURLER

". . . thunk, splatter."

2nd level archer [UNDEAD]
Initiative: +3
Vulnerability: holy

Two-handed pumpkin smash +7 vs. AC—6 damage
   Natural 16+: The target is weakened until the end of its next
      turn from having a pumpkin smashed over its head or having
      goopy pulp splatter its eyes.

Hurled pumpkin +7 vs. AC—8 damage
   Natural even hit: The target takes a −2 penalty to AC and PD
      until the end of its next turn due to being covered in goopy
      pulp. In addition, it takes a −2 penalty to Dexterity checks
      until the end of the battle (cumulative).

Headshot: A critical hit against a zombie drops it to 0 hp.

AC	15	
PD	14	**HP 50**
MD	9	

Loot: The zombies have no valuables on them. For PCs looking to take advantage of the fact that many of the square's merchants fled with only their coinpurses, they can grab small valuables worth 1d6 x 10 gp from the booths and stalls, but if they fail a DC 15 check the Shields and/or remaining townsfolk will see them and take issue. Don't bring it up yourself: this is for larcenous PCs who just can't help looting.

Aftermath: As the battle is ending (the main force of 13 zombies is down) and the crowd has mostly fled from the square, the magical whirlwind around the contact will dissipate. Then shouts will erupt from the northeastern exit. A unit of eight Silver Shields will rush into the square, cutting down any zombie mooks that are still guarding the exit. They will react in horror to the sight of the bloody scene and begin ordering people to tell them what happened as they search the area for more undead. Eventually the unit's human leader, Sergeant Parelles, will order his soldiers to take the wounded to healers as town wizards and other officials start rushing onto the scene, creating more chaos.

While the attack succeeded in creating terror and new corpses, a rash decision by a pair of Seeker agents (see lead 3) to stash a zombie in a pumpkin wagon with a carved pumpkin on its head added a bit of humor to the scene as well. Servants of the Lich King who might have been watching the attack will not be pleased with Garados' agents bungling what should have been a grand spectacle of horror, giving them yet another reason to believe that Garados is incompetent.

A JOB FOR HEROES

As the heroes recover from the battle and the town's wizards and officials arrive to sort out the mess, their contact will gather them in a corner of the square. The contact will ask them what they saw or heard during the battle, and relate how he/she/it believes someone powerful just targeted them (and thus the icon they represent) and the town's authority (in the form of the Silver Shields) with that attack. As the PCs watch Silver Shield guards pour into the square and hear them converse with the town wizards, it will quickly become obvious that the Shields are afraid, undermanned due to other issues they're also dealing with, and have no intention of acting immediately against the threat the attack represents. The wizards are caught up in their rivalries among the schools, blaming each other for the incident. In other words, they aren't going to be much help.

At that point, the PCs' contact will decide to act. He/she/it will direct the PCs to discover who was behind the attack, be *discreet* about their investigation, and, most importantly, make sure no further attacks happen. (Whether the PCs view this as bringing the guilty parties before the Silver Shields, or delivering justice themselves is up to the group.) Their contact also warns the group not to create problems for the icon he/she/it represents by falsely accusing or attacking anyone.

The contact will use whatever motivation is required to gain the PCs' help in the matter, whether it means bribery, favors from the icon, coercion (the contact refuses to provide whatever it was that the PC was coming to them for until the matter is resolved), or something else. Once the heroes agree, the contact asks them to talk to survivors in the square to see if they can learn anything while he/she/it talks to the Shields to see what they know (PCs can tag along as they wish). At this point, have the characters roll their icon relationship dice to see what leads, complications, and magical aid they might gain during this time for the upcoming adventure.

Advantages will bring information, and possibly magical aid or complications (see **Assistance from the Icons**). The information could come from things they overhear in the square, from flashback scenes where the PC was given information that didn't make sense at the time but does now, or even from agents of the other icons that arrive in the square after the attack (GM, this option might take some quick NPC creation on your part; you could use the names from the NPC contacts that weren't used). If a PC rolls an advantage for a villainous icon that they have a positive relationship with, work with the player to make the story fit why that icon's organization is helping (for example, perhaps an agent of the icon wants to gain leverage on the town's leaders). Try to embrace all the PCs' icon associations at this point.

LONG TERM CONTACTS?

Feel free to flesh out the icon contact you choose for the PCs as a long-term NPC. They could provide information and resources on future adventures. The same goes for any NPC agents of the icons you introduce at this point to give the PCs leads or aid.

ASSISTANCE FROM THE ICONS

Thanks to their connections with the icons and their organizations, the PCs probably have some inside knowledge or equipment to help them in the upcoming adventure. Advantages they roll on their icon relationship dice after the attack take the form of leads, magical aid, and possible complications. The GM should handle future icon relationship rolls (such as at the start of a new session) normally after this, though you should feel free to use any of these options later too.

- If one 5 or 6 comes up, give that PC one piece of information from the Leads options below (choose or roll).
- If two 5s and/or 6s come up, give that PC a lead and also one item from the Magical Aid options (choose an item based on the icon involved or roll randomly).
- If any PC gets three or more 5s and/or 6s, give them a second lead, and perhaps some special aid later in the adventure when the PC needs it (perhaps that icon's people are following the group to make sure the PCs is successful in the endeavor so the icon gets the credit).

- For each 5 that comes up, however, add a complication to the benefits gained. See the list of complications that follow the Lead and Magical Aid options, or create a complication that fits that PC's icon relationships.

The following leads and magical aid options are loosely broken out by icon based on their areas of influence. Feel free, however, to provide a PC with any lead or aid that fits their *unique* and story, regardless of icon relationship. **The first four leads will take the PCs to locations where they can interact with NPCs and gain information directly outlined in this adventure.** The last four leads are open-ended and can be fleshed out by a GM as desired, or re-routed back to the first four leads. If you're feeling adventurous, roll for each lead a PC gains. If not, only choose from the first four.

Each of the first four leads will take the heroes to a different part of Eldolan and, eventually, to those working for Garados or for the Seekers. Have the PCs visit at least three leads (those outlined or others you create) before they get a major clue in who was behind the attack: the name of the primary Seekers agent involved, **Arlissa Thent**, a favored subordinate of Garados. That way the PCs are likely to get into some trouble (and battles) as they learn more about what's going on.

FORESHADOWING AND SUBTLETY

One key to running this adventure is to not point the PCs at Garados and the Lamplighter's Guild too soon. Too many mentions of the guild in a negative way could lead to the PCs directly assaulting the Lanternwerks, attacking first and asking questions after everyone is dead. Try to sprinkle in descriptions of how many wizards wander around the town wearing robes of all types (both students and others) and also how the Lanternwerks wizards wear a variation of the school robes as they go about the town lighting lamps at night, making "somebody wearing wizard robes" the thinnest of clues.

LEADS

1: A half-elven woman named Elsa Whiterose, a servant of the Priestess who runs a mission in the Commons, reports that she recognized two of the zombies from the square. She claims they were poor folk who lived in the Commons and often sought food at her mission. (Priestess, GGW, Crusader)

2: Some stories have been circulating lately in the Docks that someone named Aerto is interested in buying bodies of the recently deceased and paying well for them. Perhaps there's a connection. (Dwarf King, Prince, Diabolist)

3: A tent vendor at Hawker's Square, a halfling named Rollo the Thin, recognized one of the zombies as a friend who had died a week earlier from a horse accident (broken neck). Rollo swears the man's body was laid to rest in the Dead Vaults (town crypts) in the Temple district. If that was true, how could it be walking around the square? (Emperor, Priestess, Elf Queen, Lich King)

4: One of the square vendors, a dwarven man named Rumney, says he saw two people in wizard robes actually overturn the pumpkin cart right before the attack. They had the hoods on their robes up, so he couldn't see faces or tell race (other than not small). Then one of them pointed at somebody (the contact) and that's when the trouble started. He does know who owned the pumpkin cart. (Archmage, Prince, Dwarf King, Orc Lord)

5: The stairwell that the zombies emerged from leads to a small sewer overflow chamber. The outer door to the square was unlocked and open. Inside, there's only a pair of narrow stone sewer grates. The Shields investigated the chamber and claim that the grates weren't damaged and there is no way anyone could have squeezed through them, but one of the two people who kept a key to the outer door, a Silver Shield guard named Martos, didn't show up to work today. (Emperor, Archmage, the Three)

6: A wizard student named Caleb Rosefist was performing some magical research the previous night near Hawker's Square. He reported that something disturbed his crow familiar and the square's lanterns were out. When he looked through the crow's eyes, he saw a group of robed figures moving slowly across the square and into the stairwell. Then two figures returned from the stairway, but not the others. He assumed they were up to roguish business and didn't say anything until he heard about the attack. (High Druid, Archmage, the Prince)

7: Observations of the now-dead zombies reveals that each body is missing a number of different organs, and even with the damage they sustained in the fight, that those organs were surgically removed. Not many people in town would have the knowledge to perform such surgery. (Archmage, Emperor, Priestess, Crusader)

8: People have been going missing in Eldolan for months, more so than can be accounted for through normal murders, kidnappings, and such. Whatever is going on seems to be escalating, especially in the Commons. (Crusader, Diabolist, Lich King, Orc Lord, Prince, the Three)

MAGICAL AID

1: Give out these items if the PC gets a second advantage with their starting icon rolls, or as a boon for icon relationship advantages later in the adventure. True magic items are described in chapter 9 of the *13ᵗʰ Age* core book. The *divine tears of Halatir* below is a new item described here.

2: 2 vials of **divine tears of Halatir**, patron saint of Eldolan. There are two ways to use this blessed water: apply it to a weapon or use it as a weapon. (Priestess, GGW, Crusader, Diabolist)

- Applying it to a weapon (a standard action) makes attacks with that weapon deal holy damage. The effect lasts until the end of the battle.
- Making an attack using the **divine tears of Halatir** is a standard action. **R: Dexterity or Wisdom + Level vs. PD (one nearby undead or demon enemy)**—1d6 holy damage per level.

3: 2 **Potions of Healing, adventurer-tier.** (any)

4: A **Potion of Negative Energy Resistance**. (Priestess, GGW, Crusader, Archmage, Lich King)

5: A **+1 Rune**, with the icon's symbol on it. (any)

6: A suit of **+1 Armor of Iron Will**, light or heavy. (Dwarf King, Orc Lord, Emperor)

7: A **+1 [Weapon] of Protection**, of a type (melee weapon) that the PC can use. (GGW, High Druid, Crusader, Prince)

8: A **+1 Implement/Wand of the Mage's Invisible Aegis**. (Archmage, Elf Queen, Lich King, the Three)

9: Another item of your choice that fits the PC's class and story. (any)

COMPLICATIONS

Add complications to leads or magical aid when the PCs roll one or more 5s for their icon checks.

- To get the lead information, the PCs need to visit someone "sketchy" in another part of town. (GM, feel free to ad-lib an interesting NPC encounter, perhaps with an information broker who could be useful down the road.)
- An agent of another icon the PC has a conflicted or negative relationship with, or who opposes the icon that was targeted, attempts to interfere (DCs for that PC are now 2 points higher for gaining information from NPCs, false leads are created that waste time, etc.)

- Members of the Seekers of the Lost are among those who arrived in the square, watching to see the town's reaction, and they hear about the PCs involvement. They hire a freelance halfling cutpurse named Mabs to tail the PCs to learn about their capabilities and to discover where they might be staying, allowing Garados to use this information (+2 bonus to Seekers' damage rolls vs. PCs) or plan an ambush (see **Seeker Ambush**, add one skeleton warrior). Mabs is unaware of his contacts' Seekers affiliation, but if caught he can describe them as two human men wearing wizard robes (with persuasion he might remember that they were Arcanists of the Hidden Veil robes).
- One of the items given as part of magical aid has an annoying quirk (more so than normal) that hinders the investigation in a humorous way (perhaps the wielder likes to insult people who are helping them). Or there's an NPC thief who's been waiting for a chance to steal the item and now finally will try to do so.
- One of Eldolan's other problems (see page 10) interposes itself into the PCs' investigation at some point, slowing them down and possibly leading them into a confrontation.
- A member of one of the wizard schools takes a dislike to, or is annoyed by, one of the PCs. Members of that school play dangerous pranks on the PC when they spot him or her.

FOLLOWING THE LEADS

Once the PCs gain leads from their connections, they can determine which one to follow first. If none of the PCs gain a lead from icon rolls, their contact returns after having talked to Sergeant Parelles, the Silver Shield watchman who is still in the square trying to figure out what happened. The contact will relate the only lead the Shields have, saying that a servant of the Priestess (Elsa from lead 1) recognized a few of the zombie attackers as folk from the Commons.

The icon relationship rolls assume the PCs are already talking to various people in the square, but if the heroes also want to use their skills to further question the townsfolk currently in Hawker's Square, that's fine. Reveal one additional lead to the first PC that makes a successful DC 15 skill check using Charisma (street knowledge, diplomacy), Strength (intimidation), or another ability that make sense for their method/line of questioning. Each lead will have connections to the others, however, so if the PCs only have one or two leads, it's okay.

Before the investigation into the attack truly begins, the PCs might need to handle some basic necessities such as establishing lodging and buying equipment, since they just arrived in town, or you can skip that part and get right to the action. Tracking down

the perpetrator(s) of the attacks might take some time, however, so if you want to flesh out Eldolan and its shops more to establish it as a possible home town, this would be a good time to do it.

Which lead the PCs follow is up to them. The first four leads are outlined in the following section, while the last four provide undeveloped leads you can expand as you wish. For example, perhaps the PCs track down the Silver Shield who has a key to the outer door of the overflow chamber (lead 5), and he has a connection to Aerto in a debt owed that forced him to allow the key to be copied (lead 2). Or Caleb the wizard student (lead 6) had his familiar track one of the figures he saw in the square to the Commons near the theater (Paulos, see lead 1) after they left the square. Or maybe questions about who would have the skill to perform precise surgery on people (lead 7) leads the group to a town healer, who directs the heroes to the priests at the Dead Vaults and eventually a search in the crypts for Landon. And there could be many NPCs looking for missing friends and family (lead 8) who the PCs come across in their search; those people could provide clues to any of the developed leads (leads 1–4), or possibly to a rogue group of wizard students performing experiments. Feel free to come up with options that suit your story.

ONE WAY TO USE THE LAMPLIGHTER'S GUILD

As soon as some groups of players get a sniff of Lamplighter involvement in the zombie attack or with the Seekers from some of the subtle clues found while pursuing different leads, they might decide to storm the Lanternwerks (see page 52) and sort it out later. That's one option, but not all of the guild wizards are part of the Seekers. You might want to put some doubt into the players' minds until they find stronger evidence against Arlissa that makes things more clear.

One way to do this would be to have the Lamplighters help the PCs out early in the adventure, possibly during one of the battles outside. Perhaps partway through a battle with the Ratsmashers (lead 1) or the dwarf laborers (lead 2), one of the guild wizards lights a nearby lantern, illuminating things better and raising the escalation die by +1 for the group. Or perhaps a Lamplighter lights a dark street in the Saddle when the PCs are on their way to the Dead Vaults (lead 3) or the old brewery (lead 4) and the heroes see some shadowy figures that were waiting to ambush them scurry away in fear. Putting a shadow of doubt in the players' minds might help them make the effort to determine whether the entire guild is involved in the plot or just select members. Remember, keep the players guessing!

LEAD 1:

ELSA WHITEROSE, THE COMMONS

A servant of the Priestess named Elsa Whiterose recognized two of the zombies as folk from the Commons. She runs a mission in the district.

THE COMMONS

Named after the common folk who live there, the Commons is the largest district in Eldolan and holds the most people. It contains a mix of tenement homes, small shops that cater to the poorer folk, and industry that is too loud, disruptive, or dangerous for the Saddle. The main gate into the town is set into the southern wall of the Commons, and the main road runs through the district, exiting through another wall into the Saddle not far from the entrance to the Temple district. Gaining entrance to the Saddle costs 2 cp, which keeps most of the poor folk out unless they have a workorder.

The Commons houses a handful of well-known (one way or another) areas including: Hawker's Square, the Warrens (a maze-like area of alleys and abandoned buildings that is a known thieves' den), the Alehouse Brewery (the primary dwarven brewery in town), and Tavern Row (as the name suggests, an area filled with drinking establishments for the Commons laborers, which gets very rowdy at the end of each work day).

Parts of the Commons are well lit, especially near the gates, main road, and entrance to Temples. The Lamplighters don't go into the Warrens (the lanterns are always stolen), and so the place stays in shadow. As a sign of bravery (or drunkenness), wizard students from all three schools often "slum it" at Tavern Row. They also often end up in wizard duels that do more damage to those watching than to each other.

ICON INVOLVEMENTS IN THE COMMONS

Most of the wizard students consider themselves the "betters" of those who live in the Commons, and they act like it. Wizards from all three Schools will pull magical pranks on the folk of the district. Most are harmless, though some less so.

Lately, the students have been focusing their pranks upon one group in the Commons: either the Alehouse dwarves who have connections with the Dwarf King, or a day-laborer group that is part of a union affiliated with the Emperor (or possibly the Prince). Most of the students or their families have connections to the Archmage. Some of the pranks have caused serious loss of income, and now representatives from the affected icons for those groups are getting involved. Perhaps they pull one of the PCs visiting the district into the issue, asking them to smooth things over or deal with the worst wizard offenders somehow.

ELSA WHITEROSE

Elsa Whiterose is a cleric of the Gods of Light in service to the Priestess. She runs the Mission of Lost Hope, a small organization that helps feed the poor and gives them basic shelter at night off the streets. The mission is in the Commons, near Griffin square, a small courtyard near the cliffs that separate the Commons from the Grounds above and close to the Temple district. Locals will point out its location freely.

Elsa receives a small stipend from the Priestess' organization, as well as small donations from the town's merchant class, to help keep the doors open. She has two assistants, Goram (half-orc man) and Ilsa (human female teen), who help her run the mission in exchange for small private rooms and steady meals. Between ten and twenty poor folk of various races stay at the mission at any given time. While at the mission, Goram or Ilsa might try to pressure the heroes into donating to the cause.

When questioned about the attack in Hawker's Square, Elsa can relate the following information to those who act civilly toward her. She will not give her time to those who are rude, but may suggest a small donation to the mission as a means of making up for bad behavior:

- She was in the square during the attack. She is not a fighter, but managed to hold a zombie at bay through her divine power, protecting a small group of folk trapped in one corner of the square.
- During the initial attack, she was surprised to recognize two of the attacking undead as recent poor folk who had stayed at the mission: **Tolvus Rhys**, a middle-aged human man with a bad leg from his years fighting with the legions who had a hard time finding work; and **Korack Stoneson**, a dwarven drunk who often slept one off at the mission.
- She had last seen Tolvus about ten days ago at the mission. She thinks she remembers seeing Korack about a week ago on the streets. Both Tolvus and Korack lived in the Commons, and both worked (when they could) or begged near the mission.
- The poor folk in the area have been talking about folks going missing for the last month, and she had noted a few common faces at the mission were no longer around. Although the mission has a transient population, she was worried enough to report it to the Silver Shields, but they made little effort to find those missing (because Elsa couldn't afford to make it worth their trouble). After a half day's meager search, the Shields concluded that the missing people had left town.
- There was a rumor among the poor that a pair of (human) men had been seen carrying away one of the locals known as old Ralph, even as he yelled and cursed, four days ago from an abandoned building, and that he wasn't the first. Elsa says that she only heard this second-hand, and that the PCs would have to ask around among the poor folk, and especially those on the streets, to learn more.

Talking to Streetfolk

If the PCs attempt to ask those staying at the mission about missing folk, they will get a mix of dirty looks, warning signs against evil, mad mutterings, and similar reactions, with people saying they don't want to be involved with it. A PC can make a DC 15 Charisma check (diplomacy) or Strength check (intimidation) to get a name of a street local named Riley Threefingers (not at the mission but on the streets) who might know something about Ralph. If the PC offers a small amount of money as extra incentive, they gain a +5 bonus to the check. PCs with a positive or conflicted relationship with the Priestess or Great Gold Wyrm could also use that to gain Riley's name with a successful icon relationship check (at your suggestion if they don't ask). Otherwise, after wasting half

a day asking around on the streets the PCs will get the names of one or more of the following NPCs who might know something more: Jagger Dunn, Kalia, or Riley Threefingers.

Jagger Dunn (male dwarf): Jagger can be found easily enough by asking the local street folk. He is a sometime dwarven laborer and constant drunk. He smells of stale beer, and his general appearance is grimy, with stained and threadbare clothing. When encountered, he'll probably be hanging out on a street corner, singing a tavern song and nursing a bottle of warm beer while taking a few coppers in his sweat-stained hat. Otherwise, he'll be rolled up in a blanket in an alley (pointed out by locals). Play up his drunkenness, or his bad hangover.

When questioned about those who are disappearing, Jagger can relate the following information (given the promise of a bottle or skin of something strong):

- Two weeks ago he was sleeping one off in a nearby alley during the dark hours before sunrise. A ruckus woke him up and he saw two men in robes, like those the wizard students wear, struggling with old Ralph, one of the street folk. Ralph was putting up a fight, but he was old and weak from the "cough" and then one of the men hit him in the head and it was over. Jagger stayed real quiet, knowing he would join Ralph if they noticed him. As the men were loading Ralph onto a hand cart and covering him with a blanket, one of them told the other that "he wants living subjects for the experiments now, because things have progressed." Jagger swears he wasn't that drunk when he saw this and it really happened, though most folks he told laughed at him. Further questioning (with promises of additional drink) reveals that the robed men were older, not the usual age of the wizard students who sometimes slum in the Commons taverns. He thinks the robes were gray or silver, but it was dark so he couldn't be sure.
- Jagger knew Korack (one of the zombies); the two often drank and occasionally worked as laborers together. Three days after Ralph was taken, Korack was supposed to meet Jagger at a nearby site to carry bricks for a masonry job, but never showed. Jagger cursed him for making them miss out on the coins, but now wonders if he was taken. The night before the attack Korack had mentioned that he was afraid for his life because two humans he didn't know had brought him free beer and plied him with questions about himself in an unnatural way. One of them named himself Paulos or Paully, and the other Sigmund. Jagger has never heard of Paulos/Paully, but there is a man named Sigmund new to the district. He works for some drug pusher by the old abandoned theatre.

Kalia the Waif (female half-elf): Kalia is a 14-year-old street urchin who keeps to herself instead of running with a gang. She can be found running small errands for some of the shop owners in the area, or keeping an eye on the proceeds for the various street musicians that perform in Hawker's Square. She has short, dark hair under a cap and dresses like a boy to throw off potential attackers, carries a small blade for when that doesn't work, and talks tough when cornered. For the promise of a few coins, she's willing to talk about whatever the PCs want to hear about, even though she thinks it's probably some sort of trap and will be very skittish.

When questioned about those who are disappearing, Kalia can relate the following information:

- Kalia knew Tolvus Rhys. He was a friend who had helped her one time when a couple of Ratsmasher gangers cornered her and were smashing her up with bricks. He stepped in and sent them running. Tolvus was a capable fighter, even with his bum leg, but he had a weakness for dreamleaf, a drug that produces stupors and hallucinations. Lately his shakes had been bad since he had no coin to buy the leaf. She had given Tolvus a few coppers she could spare, and he had said that he had found a new dreamleaf pusher calling himself "the Dreammaster" who was selling at half the usual rate. Kalia hasn't seen Tolvus since and it's been a week. She fears the worst, especially after the rumors about him being one of the zombies spread through the district.

- She knows that the Dreammaster runs his business out of an abandoned theatre a few blocks away. She says she's seen him once, describing him as a middle-aged human man wearing the clothes of a storekeeper, but more rumpled and dingy. She says he's new to the Commons and has been pushing for only a month or so. She also warns the PCs to be careful around him; word is that he and his thugs gutted a halfling cutpurse who tried to rob his stash.

Riley Threefingers: Riley is a scruffy, brown-haired halfling just out of youth who is a small-time local fence. He knows a few people and claims he knows more. He's wily and evasive at best, but will trade information for hard coin without a problem, as long as it won't get him in trouble with the local gangs. He tries to use big words, but doesn't always understand what they mean. If the PCs look like easy marks (no rogue types among them), he might try to pickpocket a PC while talking to them (DC 20 Wisdom check for that PC to notice; takes a small, useful, non-magical item or 1d10 coins).

When questioned about those who are disappearing, Riley can relate the following information if the PCs can make it worth his effort (a few coins or some useful info):

- He knew both Korack (a drunk) and Tolvus (a loser who used to fight for the empire) as local street folk.

- He heard about old Ralph getting taken, but he says word was that Ralph had failed to pay coin owed to a man named the Dreammaster (a drug pusher) and it was his people that grabbed the old man.

- Others have gone missing (more than normal) over the last month (he can name three more). Seems like most of them were addicts (drugs or alcohol).

- The Dreammaster is a new player in the Commons. Word is that he pays the Ratsmashers a hefty fee to operate on their turf, and that his prices are the lowest. They call him the Dreammaster because he deals dreamleaf. The Dreammaster has two dangerous thugs watching his back, at least while he's on the street: a human named Sigmund and another named Paully (or something like that). They are odd, because they often wear old wizard robes over their street clothes, but no one's ever seen them do magic.

- The Dreammaster is holed up in an abandoned building a few blocks away; it used to be a theatre years ago, before it was partially burned out. The upper floor of the place is a wreck waiting to fall, and anyone inside risks their neck with every step, but the main level is okay. There are rumors that some people who go there don't come back.

THE RATSMASHER'S TURF

At some point while the PCs are questioning street folk around the mission (and definitely before they travel to the Dreammaster), they will attract the attention of the Ratsmashers, a local gang of street toughs who claim the area. The gangers think the PCs are being too nosy and look like they have a bit of coin, and so they will try to ambush the heroes. Their leader, a human teen nicknamed Capper (real name Varlo), will confront them. While only a teen, Capper oozes charisma, speaks well, and seems to have a touch of the Prince's charm. When he tells the heroes to hand over their valuables, he does so in a tone that sounds like a knife cutting through butter—smooth.

Read to the players: *As you make your way down a narrow street filled with trash on your way to talk with a streetperson who might know something, you see a slim figure ahead leaning against a wall cleaning his fingernails with a knife. The man . . . or rather a human youth of perhaps sixteen or seventeen, turns to look at you with a smile. He says, "Greetings travelers. What a lovely band of misfits you are. I hate to trouble you, but off the beaten path as you are, well, you look like you have more than enough coins in those pouches to share. Throw me your purses now and we'll stay the best of friends."*

As he speaks, a group of tough-looking youths emerges from nearby alleyways and behind piles of trash and debris both in front of and behind you, blocking escape. Each youth holds a hand behind his or her back and is grinning wildly, revealing blackened and rotting teeth.

Capper and the PCs are in the bottleneck of a narrow alley that widens as you move away from the area in either direction. There's a T intersection with another alley 40 feet behind the PCs, and the alley in front of them goes 70 feet before intersecting with a cross street (see map opposite). The walls of the buildings framing the street are made of mortared stone bricks, but there is one locked wooden door just ahead of the PCs on the left. The buildings are 25 feet high, and there is a small balcony with locked shutters 15 feet up opposite the doorway that can hold two people. The gangers and PCs start off nearby eachother, with the street toughs coming from both directions (they came out of the alleys or were hidden in the street ahead). In addition to **Capper**, there are **two Ratsmasher brickthrowers** hiding on the balcony ready to throw bricks, and **twelve Ratsmasher street toughs** (mooks) on the street level surrounding the PCs (one mob of six on each side).

Tactics: Assuming the PCs decline Capper's offer, Capper will throw his knife on the first round as the street toughs charge forward, then he will engage a soft-looking target already engaged with his troops. As they fight, the gangers will encourage each other using their gang names (Smasher, Brickhead, Slice, Dart, Smothers, etc.).

Climbing the stone walls requires a DC 15 Strength check. Picking the lock on the door or bashing it open also requires a DC 15 check (Dex or Str); the door opens into a grain warehouse. The street toughs will intercept any PC trying to get past their ambush point or get to Capper before he takes his turn. If Capper goes down and at least six of the street toughs have dropped, at the start of each Ratsmasher's turn, that ganger must roll a normal save; on a failure, they run.

If there are only 4 PCs, remove one brickthrower. If there are 6 PCs, add four more street toughs.

Making Friends?

While the rest of the gang members are uneducated, filthy, and desperate, Capper seems to be different. Perhaps he is a noble's son who escaped to a life of freedom, an agent of an icon working the streets, or touched by the Prince's power in some way. If the PCs are willing to hand over their pouches (assume they lose 1/3 of their total money in this case) and want to befriend the gang, there's a chance they can do so.

Once he has their pouches, Capper will then ask for the heroes' weapons, since "they're all such good friends now." At that point, the PCs can try to use social skills to redirect the situation. It takes one successful DC 15 Charisma check to convince the gang to not press the issue and let the PCs keep their weapons; failure means a battle breaks out. A second successful DC 20 Charisma check will make Capper decide he likes the heroes and be willing to have his gang stand down and disperse while he talks to them. He knows the area and will be able to give them basic details about the Dreammaster and the layout of the lobby and main level of the theater, plus the fact that the upper story is unsafe. He could also be a future NPC contact for further adventures in Eldolan.

Alternately, you can let each PC that has a relationship with the Prince of Shadows make an icon relationship check to be able to win over Capper and the gang. Treat each 5 or 6 as one successful skill check, though with possible complications.

Ratsmasher Street Toughs

"What are you looking at? You want some trouble?"

1st level mook [HUMANOID]
Initiative: +3

Knife/Club/Sharpened bone +7 vs. AC—3 damage
Natural 16+: The street tough fights dirty and the target takes 2 extra damage.

Strength in numbers: A street tough gains a +1 bonus to damage if at least two other allies are engaged with the target of its attack.

AC	16	
PD	15	**HP 5 (mook)**
MD	11	

Mook: Kill one street tough mook for every 5 damage you deal to the mob.

Balcony

RATSMASHER BRICKTHROWER

"Eat this!"

1st level archer [HUMANOID]
Initiative: +3

Brick punch +5 vs. AC—2 damage

R: Hurled brick +7 (+8 for high ground) vs. AC—4 damage
Natural even hit: The target is dazed until the end of its next turn.

Superior position: A brickthrower gains a +1 bonus to AC and PD if it is on higher ground than an attacker. It also gains a +1 bonus to ranged attacks if it is on higher ground than its target.

AC	16 (17)	
PD	15 (16)	**HP 25**
MD	12	

CAPPER (RATSMASHER GANG LEADER)

"That's a really nice belt you're wearing. I bet it would really look good on me."

1st level leader [HUMANOID]
Initiative: +7

Hidden crowbar +7 vs. AC—4 damage
Natural even hit: Capper pops free from the target and can move as a free action.

R: Knife +9 vs. AC—3 damage
Limited use: 1/battle.

Get 'em!: Whenever Capper attacks, one nearby ally can make a melee attack as a free action.

AC	17	
PD	12	**HP 32**
MD	14	

Loot: Once the Ratsmashers have been defeated or sent running, the PCs can search the bodies of the fallen for valuables, though most were impoverished themselves. There is a total of 12 gp in silver and copper coins, along with various personal items of no value. Capper has the only thing of real value on him—a small bundle of dreamleaf worth 30 gp on the black market (or 15 gp if turned in to the Archmage's folk).

Aftermath: If questioned about the Dreammaster, any Ratsmashers who are captured can tell the PCs that he pays them a small fee in dreamleaf to operate in their turf, out of a nearby theater. They can give directions or lead the PCs to the building.

THE DREAMMASTER

The Dreammaster is a short, middle-aged human man in shopkeeper's rumpled clothes with graying red hair and teeth stained black from dreamleaf usage named Torsar Blacktooth. He peddles his "dreams" in the form of a drug called dreamleaf and is involved in many other black market activities. He recently moved to Eldolan from Drakkenhall in an effort to expand the dreamleaf business for his boss in that city. Whether he serves the Three (the Blue) or some other icon should depend on the PCs' story and whether icon relationships suggest it. He might be in Eldolan for other, darker purposes too.

Torsar set up his business in an old, abandoned two-story theater in the north-central Commons. The building's upper floor is a fire hazard of weak floors and poor structural integrity, but the main floor and basement of the place are solid enough. He and his people make their transactions with customers in a lobby on the main floor, and it's well-guarded against those who might think to steal from him. He keeps his inventory—and other projects—in the basement, guarded by stronger protections.

Not long after Torsar set up shop, two members of Garados' Seekers of the Lost, Sigmund and Paulos, approached the pusher. They offered to serve him for free, in exchange for his help obtaining "the dregs of society" no questions asked. Torsar accepted their help in making contacts and getting the business running, as well as with distribution, and in exchange has provided the two with some low-cost product for enticing their victims to come to the theater, where they are more easily taken. He also provides a cell in the basement of the theater where the unfortunates can be kept until the two Seekers move them to what Torsar assumes is their final destination.

APPROACHING THE THEATER

If anyone tries to climb to the upper floor from outside to get a look at the operation, the poor structural integrity of the second level makes it a tougher check (DC 20). Failure results in a crash landing back into the street for the PC attempting it and will alert those inside (but describe how dangerous it looks to the PCs before they attempt it). Even with success, moving to a position to see the main stage will require balance and stealth (DC 15 Dex check) since the boards creak and fracture. Failure results in a crash to the floor inside for 2d6 damage.

Torsar has hired a few street urchins to keep an eye out for anyone watching the theater, and they will report to him if they see the PCs taking an interest (either the PCs take no precautions or fail a DC 15 check to do so). If warned, Torsar will prepare his defenses, and given time, he might even hire a few local street thugs to deal with the PCs (have a mob of 6 street toughs intimidate/attack them outside; see the Ratsmasher battle for stats).

If the PCs watch the place for a little while, they will see customers coming and going.

The main level of the theater is divided into three sections: the front entrance, which consists of a small lobby and a ticket cage; the main stage and auditorium seating; and the backstage storerooms. There is also a cellar containing the holding cell and Torsar's stash. See map, page 24.

FRONT LOBBY

A pair of double doors allow access into the small (30 by 20 foot) lobby from outside (but one of the doors has been nailed shut), and two sets of double doors lead from there to the stage. Most buyers, however, aren't allowed beyond the lobby. **Four street thugs** (half-orc, 3 humans) guard the lobby, two by each set of double doors. The ticket cage is made from strong oak with iron bars on the top half, and has a small wooden side door that is bolted from the inside. Within the cage, a halfling named **Jarsil Ralss** passes his time playing solitaire, insulting the thugs, and selling merchandise when a buyer comes into the lobby. The guards closely watch anyone entering to buy, and if more than two people come in, they will instruct the others to "wait outside or they'll get a beating." Any trouble (such as more than two people entering and not leaving) brings a quick and violent response; this might not alert those beyond the doors unless a thug flees to the main stage, there are abnormally loud magical explosions, or the escalation die reaches 3, since deadbeats get beaten and thrown out of the lobby at least once a day.

If a buyer seeks to make a large purchase, or wants to deal with the Dreammaster personally, a show of coin and the right words (DC 15 Charisma check) can get them inside to the main stage to meet with Torsar and his people (but they still won't allow more than two people into the building this way). If the PCs go in to scout the place out and don't make a purchase, Jarsil might sniff them out and order the thugs to attack anyway (DC 15 Charisma check for the PCs to convince him, if needed).

Read to the players: *You enter through the outer doors into a small lobby. There are two sets of double doors leading into the interior of the theater, each guarded by a pair of thugs. A halfling in a wood and iron cage to your right says,*

"Let's see your coin, friends." His words ooze seediness, and his lips are curled in anticipation.

Tactics: If things go bad (like the PCs don't want to buy and won't leave, or more than two of them try to enter and don't leave), the thugs and Jarsil will use violence to put an end to the problem. If there are PCs outside the main door, it takes one move action to open the heavy door. Jarsil will target enemy spellcasters or ranged attackers with his light crossbow while the thugs work in pairs against a single foe. The ticket cage increases Jarsil's AC and PD by +4 while he's in it, so he doesn't mind taking an opportunity attack for firing the crossbow (AC 24 total). A PC can force or jimmy the cage door as a move action with one DC 20 check or two DC 15 checks, allowing one person to access Jarsil without the AC/PD penalty. Each thug will try to flee (50/50 whether they go inside or outside) on their turn once they go under 10 hp if at least half of them are already down.

Drop each thug's hp by 5 if there are 4 PCs. If there are 6 PCs, add two street thugs by the front door. If the PCs choose to take the fight through the doors into the auditorium during battle, then they will have a much harder fight on their hands including both groups of enemies (consider having Torsar, Sigmund, and Paulos show up a round or two later). If alerted, those at the main stage will prepare, but they won't join the battle in the lobby.

JARSIL RALSS (HALFLING)

"You gotta pay to play, friend!"

3rd level archer [HUMANOID]
Initiative: +7

Dagger +7 vs. AC—7 damage

R: Light crossbow +9 vs. AC—9 damage, and the target is weakened (save ends)
Limited use: 3/battle; Jarsil has coated three bolts with dreamleaf extract, and he will fire those bolts first. Afterward, his *light crossbow* attack is at-will but will do normal damage only.

Small: Jarsil gains a +2 bonus to AC against opportunity attacks.

AC	18 (22)	
PD	16 (20)	**HP 36**
MD	14	

STREET THUGS

"Let's see your coin!"

1st level troop [HUMANOID]
Initiative: +3

Beat stick +5 vs. AC—7 damage
Natural even hit: The street thug can make a *dazing blow* attack against the target as a free action.

[Special trigger] **Dazing blow +6 vs. PD**—The target is dazed (save ends).

AC	17	
PD	14	**HP 29**
MD	11	

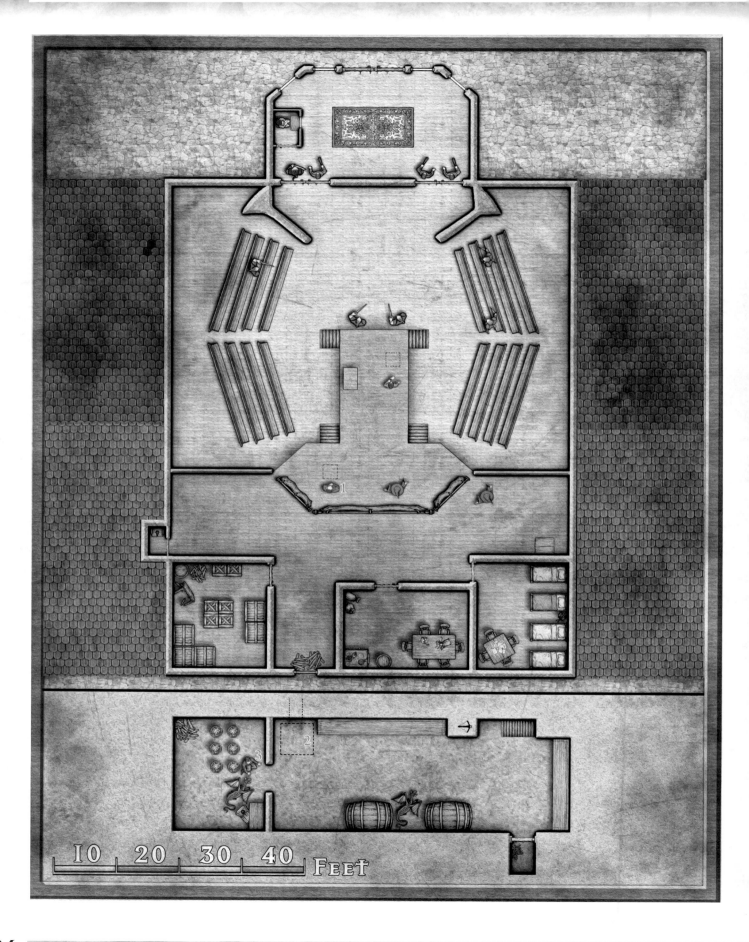

10   20   30   40   Feet

Loot: Each thug has 2d6 gp in mixed coins. Jarsil has a small cashbox in the cage holding 200 cp, 100 sp, and 50 gp, and ten small dreamleaf packages (worth 3 gp each in the black market; half that to the Archmage's folk).

Aftermath: The doors to the main stage are closed but unlocked. The sounds of battle may have alerted Torsar and his allies, however, if it was overly loud or if the battle lasted more than three rounds. Any thugs that fled will also be part of the main stage group.

Main Stage and Auditorium

The stage is made from wood and forms a T at the back with a few small raised wooden platforms on top of it and two different trapdoors in the floor to a low walkway underneath that the actors once used for performances. The walkway leads backstage. There are five close rows of stadium benches with aisles separating them in a half circle facing the stage. Three open archways covered with dusty black sheets parted in the middle separate the room from the backstage area. Many ropes and stage props are located around the periphery of the stage (good for stunts).

Tactics: Currently, **six lackeys** (3 humans, 2 half-elves, and a halfing) are lounging in the place, eating, drinking, and gambling. Sigmund and Paulos are meeting with Torsar in a backstage storeroom they've converted to a living quarters and larder. If alerted by the battle in the lobby, they will immediately move to the stage area. Torsar will also move to the main stage area, directing three lackeys to hide among the benches, while the other three move to the front of the stage. **Paulos** will hide in an archway behind a sheet with his crossbow ready. **Torsar** and **Sigmund** will move to the back of the stage with the lackeys between them and any enemies. Otherwise, they will emerge onto the stage as soon as they hear trouble in the auditorium.

Torsar has adjusted the stage engineering in his favor and each round he can throw a lever or pull on a rope as a standard action attack using the stage (a beam drops from the ceiling, a floor panel slams into a PC, etc.)—see *stage attack* in his stat block.

If things don't go well and Torsar would drop to 0 hit points, his *trapdoor escape* ability will allow him to escape to the basement (see stat block). A pressure switch makes the trapdoor shut and lock when someone hits bottom. When Torsar leaves, each lackey has a 50% chance of fleeing each round during its turn. Sigmund and Paulos will fight to the death knowing that their capture will force the Seekers to kill them anyway. Each uses the same stat block, though keep track of their hit points separately. Only Paulos has a crossbow.

If there are only 4 PCs, remove three lackeys. If there are 6 PCs, add four more lackeys, who rush in from a backstage archway.

BARDS ON STAGE

If any of the PCs are bards, they might have an easier time of it navigating the stage and its props since that's terrain with which they are intimately familiar. Bard PCs gain a +2 bonus to all defenses against Torsar's *stage attack*, and a bard can roll a save at the start of each of their turns. On a success, they can use a stage attack that turn as a standard action. Also feel free to give them a +2 bonus to any sort of dicey checks they make using the scenery.

LACKEYS

"We've got the best stuff in town!"

1ˢᵗ level mook [HUMANOID]
Initiative: +3

Knife or club +6 vs. AC—4 damage
  Natural 18+: The next creature to attack the target this battle gains a +2 bonus to attack and damage.

AC	17	
PD	15	HP 7 (mook)
MD	11	

Mook: Kill one lackey mook for every 7 damage you deal to the mob.

SIGMUND/PAULOS

"You stuck your nose where it don't belong!"

2ⁿᵈ level spoiler [HUMANOID]
Initiative: +8

Sharpened shiv +7 vs. AC—7 damage
  Natural 16+: The target takes 3 extra damage.
  Miss: 3 damage.

R: Light crossbow +7 vs. AC—7 damage (Paulos only)

Cheap shot: When Sigmund/Paulos hit a target that is engaged with at least one of their allies, the target takes +1d8 extra damage from the attack.

AC	18	
PD	15	HP 34
MD	13	

TORSAR BLACKTOOTH, THE DREAMMASTER

"You're not long for this world, fool!"

3ʳᵈ level leader [HUMANOID]
Initiative: +6

Light mace +8 vs. AC—9 damage
Natural 16+: The target is dazed (save ends).

C: Refined dreamleaf powder +7 vs. PD (one enemy engaged with Torsar)—3 psychic damage, and the target is weakened (save ends)
First failed save: The target is confused instead of weakened (save ends).
Limited use: 2/battle, as a quick action.

C: Stage attack +7 vs. PD (one nearby enemy)—6 damage, and the target is dazed or stuck (GM's choice) until the end of its next turn

Boss's tricks: Torsar's allies gain a +2 attack bonus against enemies affected by a condition Torsar created (confused, dazed, stuck, weakened).

Trapdoor escape: When an attack would drop Torsar to 0 hit points, as a free action, he instead heals to 5 hit points and negates any conditions on him, then escapes to the basement by pulling a lever that opens a trapdoor/slide in the floor next to him and leaping down it. The trapdoor locks behind him.

AC	18	
PD	15	**HP 48** (see *trapdoor escape*)
MD	13	

Loot: Each lackey has 1d4 x 10 sp. Sigmund and Paulos keep nothing of value at the theater. Each does wear a well-used wizard robe over his clothing. Paulos wears a tattered blue Eldritch Masters robe. Sigmund wears a dark blue (Lamplighter's) robe that has a very faded Lamplighter's Guild patch (a lantern) on one shoulder. Paulos also bears the Lich King's symbol branded upon the flesh over his heart (but under his clothing).

Aftermath: When Torsar escapes down the slide, there's no easy way to follow him (the lever doesn't work a second time, breaking through the wooden trapdoor will take half a minute barring extraordinary actions by the PCs, and the stairs down are backstage). He is out of the battle and will have to be dealt with later.

SIGMUND AND PAULOS

Sigmund is a tall, somewhat meaty human man with a pockmarked face and shaggy brown hair. He has a gruff voice, though he doesn't speak much. Paulos is a small, rat-faced human man with glaring eyes and short-cropped dirty blond hair. He has a wicked smile and speaks quickly with a limited vocabulary, repeating the ends of his sentences. Each wears simple well-worn clothing under their threadbare robes. Neither will mention Garados or the Seekers if somehow captured (and will meet a sudden, unexpected end if imprisoned somewhere for questioning).

BACKSTAGE STOREROOMS

There are three backstage storerooms, plus a latrine and an obvious trapdoor in a hallway floor that opens to reveal a set of stairs going down to the cellar. One storeroom is filled with old construction materials from the theater days and other debris. The other two have been converted into living quarters and a simple kitchen/eating area. The living quarters holds food, drink, a pouch with 20 gp, and 3 packets of dreamleaf worth 30 gp each on the black market (or half that as a reward if handed over to the Archmage's people).

There is also a back exit from the theater, but it's boarded and nailed shut, with a pile of debris stacked against it from the inside.

THE CELLAR

The cellar is divided into three areas: the cask room, a small brick cell, and a dreamleaf storage room.

Cask Room: Whether the PCs descend to the cellar via the slide or the stairs, they will enter into the cask room, named for two huge empty casks resting along one wall. The theater used to store spirits there to serve patrons, but now it serves another purpose.

Tactics: If the heroes use the stairs to the cellar, there is a triple crossbow trap they must deal with. Behind the stone wall at the base of the stairs before they turn into the room is a shelf set with three loaded crossbows. Unless detected, the first PC going down the stairs will trigger a pressure plate on a step near the bottom, and the crossbows will fire bolts through small holes in the wall. **Triple crossbow trap:** DC 15 to notice pressure plate and holes (if a PC is searching); **+5 vs. AC (1d3 different enemies on the stair)**—1d10 damage.

No matter which entrance into the cellar the heroes take, an **injured Torsar** and his pets—**two black drakes**—will be waiting to attack them. Torsar, now healed back to just more than half hit points, will be hiding behind the archway that leads to the storage room, along with one of the drakes. The other drake is waiting for Torsar's signal to attack (a whistle) and hidden between the casks. The first PC fully into the room can make a DC 15 Wisdom check to notice the ambush, otherwise injured Torsar and the drake by the casks will surprise the PCs, each making one attack (the drake moves to the nearest PC) before the heroes roll initiative. The second drake will wait near Torsar to intercept any enemies moving to engage him. If the PCs detect the ambush, adjust the read aloud text accordingly.

Read to the players: *You enter into the theater's cellar, which holds two large ten-foot-diameter wooden casks in racks along one wall, and some smaller wooden racks going from floor to ceiling that look like they are meant to hold wine bottles, though they are empty. A heavy wooden door with a large iron bar thrown across it exits out one corner of the room, and the opposite wall contains a dark archway. You notice a sweet, musty smell filling the room as a whistle suddenly sounds from the archway, followed by the twang of a crossbow; then something dark and quick leaps out of the shadows toward you with a snarl.*

Torsar thinks the PCs are rivals out to claim his product and will fight to the death, unless the PCs give him a way out and he believes them. As the battle winds down, however, it will suddenly get worse. In his service to Garados and the Lich King, Paulos underwent a terrible ritual. Upon his death, he will transform into a wight within a short time (but will seem dead until then). At the start of the round after Torsar drops to 0 hp (or surrenders), **Paulos the wight** will open the slide trapdoor from above (or drop down through the opening if it was broken open by the PCs) and leap into the room. If Torsar is surrendering, the wight will use his first attack to tear out Torsar's throat (no attack roll needed). Otherwise, the wight will attack a cleric in the group or the PC with the lowest hit points (with a +2 bonus to his first attack due to surprise and ferocity). He will continue to try to attack his initial target for the rest of the battle (but won't take opportunity attacks to do so).

Paulos the wight will taunt the PCs in its dry, undead voice and tell them that they "interfere with powers beyond their reckoning" as it attacks them. If a PC bears some signs of service to the Lich King, Paulos won't attack them, but will ask them to help. If there are only 4 PCs, remove one of the drakes. If there are 6 PCs, give Torsar full hit points.

BLACK DRAKES

"Snap, snap!"

2ⁿᵈ level troop [BEAST]
Initiative: +5

Snapping jaws +7 vs. AC—6 damage
Natural 16+: The target also takes 3 ongoing acid damage.

Acidic blood: While the drake is staggered, when an enemy is engaged with it at the start of its turn, that enemy takes 2 acid damage.

AC	18	
PD	16	**HP 36**
MD	11	

INJURED TORSAR

"Who are you idiots, anyway?"

3ʳᵈ level leader [HUMANOID]
Initiative: +6

Light mace +8 vs. AC—9 damage
Natural 16+: The target is dazed (save ends).

R: Heavy crossbow +8 vs. AC—11 damage
Natural even hit: Torsar whistles a command to one of the drakes, which can make a *snapping jaws* attack as a free action.
Natural odd hit: The target takes 5 ongoing damage.

Boss's tricks: Torsar's allies gain a +2 attack bonus against enemies affected by a condition Torsar created (dazed, ongoing damage).

AC	18	
PD	15	**HP 30**
MD	13	

PAULOS THE WIGHT

"My master will control you soon enough!"

4ᵗʰ level spoiler [UNDEAD]
Initiative: Goes before anyone else at start of round after Torsar dies/surrenders
Vulnerability: holy

Life-stealing claws +9 vs. AC (2 attacks)—5 damage
Natural even hit or miss: Unless the wight is staggered, the attack also deals 5 ongoing negative energy damage.

Unnatural maneuver: Twice per battle (once per round) as a free action, the wight can wretch its body in an unnatural way to gain a +5 bonus to disengage checks that turn.

AC	20	
PD	16	**HP 45**
MD	13	

Loot: Torsar has a pair of 30 gp silver rings, one on each thumb, and wears silver necklace with a small silver bear's claw on the end; it's a magical **Bearclaw Necklace** (*13ᵗʰ Age* core book, page 290). The rest of his wealth is in the dreamleaf storage room.

Brick Cell: The door to the brick cell is thick wood and has a heavy iron bar on the outside. Inside is a 4 by 7 foot mortared brick room that smells of blood and feces. Scratch marks on the door and fresh stains show that the now empty cell held someone recently.

Dreamleaf Storage Room: This 20 by 15 foot chamber has a table and chair against one wall, two piles of debris in one corner where the drakes nested, and six strands of dreamleaf hanging from the ceiling where they are drying. Once dried (another two days), each strand of dreamleaf is worth 50 gp in the black market (half that if turned over).

Aftermath: On the desk is ink, quills, a pouch of 30 gp, and a small book of debts and other payment information from Torsar's customers. In one section listed "other profits" there are three different dates entered over the last month that show payments made to Torsar for "cell fees and body delivery" paid by Paulos, with a note next to it in Torsar's writing that says, "*Follow up on rumor about someone named Aerto in the Docks paying well for destitutes, no questions asked. Might be able to leverage another buyer against Paulos and his boss to increase profits. Unless they're working together?*"

If the group is ready for the next stage of their search, you could instead change the book debt note to show payment for the delivery by Arlissa Thent (from the Lamplighter's Guild in the Saddle).

LEAD 2:

AERTO'S DEAD BODIES, THE DOCKS

Someone named Aerto has been offering good coin for freshly dead bodies in the Docks district.

THE DOCKS

One of the more dangerous parts of Eldolan, the Docks includes the port and main piers, numerous warehouses, fish processing buildings, and fishing shacks, and an array of shady taverns and inns where sailors and travelers just arrived to the city often stay. Many dark stories come out of the district, and though sailors tend to exaggerate, some are true. The transient nature of the population in the Docks makes it hard to prove or disprove the stories, and the Silver Shields have pulled back all night patrols due to recent events, though they are still patrolling the main thoroughfares in force during the day.

As a port town, Eldolan has three main piers where large ships and trading vessels can dock. There are also many shorter piers for the smaller ships, and the protected bay allows the fishermen to simply leave their craft anchored offshore around the bay's edges a short swim away. There are many open stalls selling fresh seafood near the harbor, interspersed with other small tent vendors and similar folk selling all manner of goods to those arriving via ship.

In addition to the sailors of all races who spend time in the Docks, a large contingent of dwarven laborers live and work in the district (carrying cargo off ships to the warehouses). They tend to be rough and rowdy, at the least. A number of taverns and inns line the harbor, serving sailors, travelers, and locals alike. These establishments tend to be rowdy, though a few of the larger ones keep things civil enough to draw recently arrived travelers to them (at least on the first night).

AERTO'S STORY

Aerto is a half-elf who works in the shadows, acting as a middleman in shady deals and illegal commerce of all types. He's also a member of the Seekers of the Lost who procures whatever the group needs, though he keeps that affiliation well-hidden. Aerto's elven heritage is dark elf, and the cruelness of that culture runs in him as well,

ICON INVOLVEMENTS IN THE DOCKS

Over the last few months, someone (possibly agents of the Diabolist) has been slowly distributing strange gold coins in the district. The coins feel oily to the touch and have a shark's head imprint upon them, but the gold in them is heavy. The coins were readily accepted at first, but lately stories have been circulating among the sailors patronizing the district that the coins are cursed—they've come from sahuagin hoards looted from the Midland Sea. There has been a lot of bad luck going around for those holding the coins, possibly supporting the sailors' mutterings.

Recently, the warehouse owners in the Docks (Emperor) have been trying to unload all of their "shark coins" as they call them onto the dwarven laborers who work the docks (Dwarf King). After a rash of injuries and accidents, the dwarves stopped accepting the coins, sparking pay disputes. Making matters worse, somebody had been making counterfeit shark coins while they were popular (the Prince), and no one in the Docks is accepting them anymore. Those who have the coins are unloading them on newcomers to the area (like the PCs) at bargain rates. Perhaps the PCs acquire some of the cursed coins, or try to unload them on a tavern owner in the district, and it brings trouble.

though his ability to lie with ease helps hide the trait. He speaks in a smooth but low voice that's almost a whisper, and he's always looking for an angle to improve his standing.

Aerto was recruited into the Seekers two years ago, but only recently began acquiring "materials" (bodies) for Garados' latest project. At first, it was the body of the occasional sailor or traveler who made a bad choice and ended up dead in an alley. Lately, Garados' need has increased, and so Aerto's activities have grown more bold. The bodies don't need to be cold, just passed out or incapacitated, for him to take them.

Recently, however, there has been a new development that has filled Aerto's pouch with coin but forced him to be even less discreet. A group of Diabolist cultists approached him about providing them with fodder for their rites, the fodder being humanoid corpses. Aerto saw no reason that he couldn't serve both himself and the Seekers, figuring the cult would provide him with an out in case the Shields came sniffing around. And so he put the word out that those willing to make some coin could let him know about the unfortunate recent dead instead of contacting the guard to haul the body to the town crypts.

FINDING AERTO

Finding Aerto will take a bit of legwork by the heroes. He works in the shadows and is relatively careful, but he also needs bodies, so he's open to meeting people he doesn't necessarily know to that end. The PCs will need to visit the harbor taverns and inns, the piers full of sailors and dockworkers, and perhaps some of the back alleys and warehouses in the district (if you prefer) to track Aerto down.

While talking to different NPCs, the PCs can use Charisma checks (diplomacy, bluff), Strength checks (intimidation), or other checks that seem appropriate to find him. The DC is 15, and it takes three successful checks, each with a different NPC (and possibly by different PCs if you want to get more of the players involved), to discover Aerto's current location.

Any PCs that have a relationship with the Prince of Shadows, Dwarf King, or Diabolist can roll their icon relationship dice, since the Docks district is an area where the icons have some influence. Each advantage allows the PCs to reroll one failed skill check as a contact comes forward with information, or can count as one successful check (but still requires the PCs to talk to additional NPCs). If any PC rolls a 5, however, the group will have to deal with some extra trouble during their search in the form of a group of drunk dwarven laborers (or another complication of your creation that fits the character based on their story).

Depending on the rolls (and number of failures), the PCs search for Aerto can take anywhere from a few hours to a few days. (Even with failures they will find him, but if they have three failed skill checks before three successes, he will hear that somebody is looking for him and be prepared with his story, making any checks to see through his lies require a DC 25.) When the PCs get their third success, set the time of day as after sunset, and have the NPC tell the heroes that they saw Aerto at the *Squirming Mermaid* tavern fifteen minutes ago. Of course, feel free to have the PCs talk to as many NPCs as you prefer to find Aerto instead of rolling checks, if that suits your game.

Here are a few NPC options, in no particular order, to have the PCs interact with (feel free to come up with some others). They can be affiliated with any of the icons you wish, or none:

- **Michale Orlevy:** Michale is a human scoundrel and bard who plies his trade at many of the taverns in the Docks. He is slim, red-haired, and moves with a bit of limp. Originally from New Port, Eldolan has been his home for the last two years, but it hasn't been as profitable as he'd hoped and his well-worn clothes and unpolished lute show it. The PCs encounter Michale at the *Lusty Dolphin* tavern, and for a few coins he will provide them with three or four locations in the district where he's seen Aerto.

- **Malice Sureshot:** Malice probably has another name, but no one knows what it might be. She is a thin, wiry halfing woman with short-cropped jet black hair and a hard edge about her, perhaps due to her dragon tattoos. She looks to be about thirty and wears a form-fitting green leather jerkin with black leather pants, and carries a number of sharp-looking blades on a bandolier. She will not be intimidated by the PCs, but is willing to tell the PCs a couple of locations where they can find Aerto for a "mug of good stuff" if they plan on giving Aerto trouble because "she owes him." The PCs can find her at the *Wild Wave Inn* taproom.

- **Travan Orcslayer:** Travan is a crusty, older dwarf whose brown hair has gone mostly white. He bears a few nasty scars, including one that took off his right ear, and has the look of a long-time mercenary. He won't talk to half-orcs, and will be intentionally rude to elves, but he did some work for Aerto a few weeks back and is willing to name a couple of places where Aerto likes to drink for a few coins, or for free to a dwarf who buys him a mug. He can be found singing old battle songs at the *Dwarves' Home Alehouse*, a dwarven drinking establishment.

- **Talina Brighteyes:** Talina is a golden-haired half-elven woman of indeterminable "middle-age" who tends bar at the *Westwind* tavern. She has a smile in her voice as she welcomes people into the tavern, but can also cuss with the best sailors and has a nasty temper that comes out if anyone is messing with her bar or her servers. Most of the clientele will back her if she has a problem with someone. She takes a particular liking to wood elves, but won't say more than three words to high elves.

- **Jiggs:** Jiggs is a dirty, bedraggled, older gnome man with crazy eyes. He was once an adventurer, but he saw something in the underworld that left him partially mad. Now he is a fetcher and mopper at the *Sailor's Respite* tavern, one of the more rowdy establishments on the harbor. The clientele at the *Respite* treat Jiggs like a mascot who's the butt of jokes, receiver of shoves, and target of pranks, but he's their mascot, so any outsider trying to do the same will not be looked well upon. He also fetches drinks, cleans up messes, and runs errands, all with a silly smile on his dirty face. But Jiggs sees and hears things, and if someone is nice to him, he will tell them (in a roundabout way with a lot of additional details) that he saw Aerto "a little while ago," although for Jiggs that could be ten minutes or ten days.

ALTERCATION ON THE PIER

During their search for Aerto, if the PCs fail a skill check (or get a 5 on an icon relationship check), they will run into some trouble. The trouble comes in the form a band of drunk and rowdy dwarf dockworkers that cross the heroes' path. (Alternately, if the PCs are causing trouble, it can be from a group related to the NPC they're currently talking to and set in the establishment that person is at.

For example, thugs at the *Lusty Dolphin*; halfling rogues at the *Wild Wave*; dwarf dockworkers at the *Alehouse*; mixed patrons at the *Westwind*; or drunk sailors at the *Respite*. If some other type of group makes better sense for your story based on the PCs' icon connections and *uniques*, feel free to adjust the flavor of the altercation accordingly, though the laborer stats will still work.

As the PCs are moving around the harbor seeking Aerto (preferably in the early evening hours), they will be crossing a section of pier with open water on one side and the long wall of a wooden fish processing building on the other, making for a relatively narrow passage about ten feet wide. Coming from the other direction is a group of **six dwarf laborers** who are off shift, have been drinking, and are eager to get to their next drinking establishment. As the PCs start to cross, one of the dwarves notices a magic item a PC is carrying and sees how unkept it is. The dwarf stops in front of the hero, points a figner at him or her, and says, "*You don't deserve to carry such a lovely [item] treating it that way. Have you no shame?*"

Preferably, the dwarf will choose a PC with an item who rolled a complication (a 5) with an icon check following this lead, or who failed a skill check while trying to track down Aerto. If the PCs don't have a magic item, the dwarf will comment on a mundane weapon. The dwarf's friends then get into the action, and things start to get ugly. If the heroes try to calm the dwarves and talk their way out of it, the PC with the item and one other character will need to make a DC 18 check to do so. A failure, or any insult (or perceived insult) directed toward the dwarves will bring violence on their part (and perhaps a free roundhouse to start things off).

Of course, if you want to run a battle at this point, it could be that an enemy of the heroes with icon connections paid the dwarves to waylay the PCs and they used the "you're not taking good enough care of your magic items" line to instigate it. In that case, it's a fight no matter what. The dwarves might or might not be able to describe who paid them off, if questioned, depending on how much you want them to know.

Tactics: Since there's no law in the form of Silver Shields currently around on the docks at night, the dwarves have no problem using more than fists. They fight with clubs, mugs, bricks, handy pieces of lumber, and whatever bashing weapon is at hand. (If the PCs mention not wanting to deal killing blows, however, the dwarves also won't attack anyone who's unconscious.)

The water off the end of the pier is deep enough that anyone falling/jumping off won't be harmed (assuming they can swim). There's a wood ladder leading eight feet back up to the pier. The pier also holds barrels, coils of rope, and other items one might expect in such a location.

If there are only 4 PCs, remove one laborer. If there are 6 PCs, add two laborers.

Dwarf Laborers

"Look at the grime and blood all over it!"

1ˢᵗ level troop [HUMANOID]
Initiative: +3

Makeshift weapon +6 vs. AC—6 damage
   Natural 16+: The dwarf shoves the target away and pops free from it. If the target is next to the edge of the pier, it must roll a normal save; on a failure, it falls into the bay, requiring two move actions to climb back to the pier and enter the battle.

Drunken brawlers: When an attacker scores a crit against a dwarf laborer, the laborer can immediately roll a hard save (16+). On a success, it only takes normal damage (too drunk to notice).

<u>Nastier Specials</u>
If this battle happens after the PCs have a few incremental advances under their belts, you could give the laborers the following ability:

Lucky roundhouse: When the laborer rolls a natural odd hit with a *makeshift weapon* attack, the target must immediately roll a normal save. On a failure, the target is knocked unconscious (save ends).

AC	17	
PD	16	**HP 30**
MD	10	

Loot: The dwarf laborers carry only their days' wages; each has 2d10 sp in silver and copper coins.

Aftermath: If the PCs choose to fight to the death, victory might bring more trouble as word of it spreads. Dwarves in the district will not be happy with them, justified or not, and all DCs involving dwarves increase by 3. If the dwarves were paid to fight

---

Running a Bar Fight

There's a decent chance that one of the PCs will want to start something at one of the locations in the Docks district. When this happens, instead of having to run a full battle, here's a way to simplify things.

If the PCs start a bar fight (whether from being taunted by patrons, someone's *unique* or magic item quirk lending itself to that activity, or even if the group is just spoiling for some action, go with skill checks. After someone throws the first punch, have each player tell you how their character is approaching the fight and assign a skill check for their PC based on that method (so Str for bashing heads, Con for shrugging off blows, Dex for avoiding blows, Int for using

superior tactics/positioning, Wis for seeing a weakness of the opponents, Cha for directing opponents elsewhere, etc. A DC of 15 probably works, or higher if circumstances suggest the group is in over their heads. No matter the rolls, the PCs will win the fight of course, but those who fail the check will pay a cost: they lose a recovery.

And if one of the PCs chooses to pull/use a weapon, then the bar fight becomes a battle and the opponents will also draw weapons (use the dwarf laborer stats, but make it clear initially that the opponents are looking to brawl with fists and mugs not weapons).

the PCs, they only know that some man in blue-gray wizard robes and a hood gave them each a gp to do so (and increase the loot by 6 gp). They didn't see his face.

MEETING AERTO

After talking to people in the district (and making the third successful check), the PCs will get a line on Aerto's location at the *Squirming Mermaid* tavern. When the PCs arrive, Aerto will be doing business inside. Have the PCs locate him as evening is setting in.

THE SQUIRMING MERMAID

The *Mermaid* is a shady tavern on the eastern edge of the harbor frequented by black market dealers and those who like the shadows. It's a two-story wooden structure with numerous additions that have extended the ground floor haphazardly, with some sections hanging precariously over the edge of the pier it's built upon. This ramshackle architecture has created many cubby holes and side rooms where private business can happen without too much eavesdropping. There are also four different exits (at least) from the place besides the front door.

The tavern is owned and run by Scarlet Ylas, a high elf woman with a hard frown and a dangerous stare that has sent many a rowdy patron running for the street. Rumors say that she was a ship captain in the past, and that she did a bit of pirating in

her time. The tavern reflects her personality, hard but mysterious, with many unique pieces of art from lands all around the Midland Sea. The *Squirming Mermaid* is known for its overpriced but effective liquors. They also serve a cheaper, weaker beer called "the Swill" and usually have a simple yet surprisingly flavorful fish stew in the pot.

QUESTIONING AERTO

When the PCs enter the tavern, Aerto will be in a back corner of the room talking business with a jowly, dog-faced looking human man. If the PCs ask for him, Scarlet will nod toward Aerto but say, "*I don't like trouble in my place, strangers. Keep it civil or I'll send you into the bay!*" Impress upon the PCs that the threat seems to be more than just words. If the PCs press her on the point or insult her or do harm to her tavern or her servers (if patrons get into a dispute she'll tell them to take it outside), Scarlet is not without resources. She'll give a whistle and offer a week's worth of free drinks to those who help her teach the PCs a lesson if they don't back down, and a group of shady patrons will step up (see sidebar).

Aerto will take notice of anyone using his name, but since he's someone who deals with people (and is in need of more "product"), he's willing to talk to anyone who doesn't look like a Silver Shield. Depending on how the PCs broach the subject of the bodies, Aerto will either clam up quick, or he will dance around the topic, suggesting that if they were to know where the recently deceased might be, there could be good money for them. Putting Aerto at ease and/or getting him on the topic of the deceased might require a DC 15 Charisma check (diplomacy or bluff), or can fall fully under roleplaying if the group is comfortable with banter.

If questions move in the direction of what Aerto is doing with the bodies, he will grow quiet and simply say that it's his business and the pay is good, but questions like that are not good for business. If the PCs botch it, Aerto will quickly begin to suspect that they aren't looking to sell and might be trouble, at which point he will suggest that the bodies rumor is simply a misunderstanding—he is someone who procures things for people, and he may have made a mistake in the past dealing in the dead, but no more. He will then try to leave.

If the PCs play up the fact that they have bodies to offer, Aerto will negotiate a deal with them, paying 10–15 gp per corpse. Assuming the PCs make good on the deal, Aerto will deliver the bodies to the cultists' warehouse (see below) if the PCs would think to follow him.

If the PCs continue to press him about what the bodies are for or look like they're going to become violent if they don't get answers, Aerto will play his trump card, throwing the cultists to the wolves (so to speak) without saying anything about the Seekers. He might ask for a few coins to sell the ruse as well. He will tell the PCs that a human man named Jeskill approached him a few weeks ago about procuring the recently deceased, and he was willing to pay well for bodies no questions asked. So Aerto put the word out. He will (seemingly) reluctantly tell the PCs where Jeskill is located, at an old brick warehouse at the eastern edge of the Docks district near the cliffs that lead up to the overlooking Grounds. He will proclaim that he knows nothing more (and is such a good liar that those watching for such deceit need a DC 20 check to discern that he's holding something back). If the PCs challenge Aerto's claim, he will throw them off by saying that he thinks Jeskill might be a Diabolist-worshiper (some things he overheard)! If they still don't believe him, he won't say more, being more afraid of Garados.

Once Aerto has chosen this path, he will become helpful, wanting only to get away from the PCs. He will show them the warehouse if they ask, but as soon as he has a chance, he will make himself scarce, holing up for the next week in a safe house to avoid the wrath of the cultists if they end up defeating the heroes, or if the heroes win, to avoid more questions.

Whether Aerto leads the PCs to the warehouse, intentionally or not, or gives them directions, have the PCs initially arrive at the place in the late hours of the day when it's dark.

THE CULT OF THE DIABOLIST

Aerto's false lead brings a cult of the Diabolist to the heroes' attention.

CULTIST WAREHOUSE

The warehouse is a two-story brick structure built against the stone cliffs that extend upward to the Grounds district where the Schools of Magic are located. From the outside, it looks like a simple storage facility for grains and other food items that come through the port from destinations around the Midland Sea. If the PCs decide to wait and come back to the warehouse during daylight hours, Jeskill and the other cultists will look like simple laborers hauling goods in and out of the place, though their workday starts and ends late.

The warehouse has two obvious exits: a pair of large wooden doors that open wide enough for a wagon, and a single smaller door near the side of the building (see map opposite). There are also a handful of high, narrow windows near the roofline facing the street. Although it won't be easily viewable from the outside, the warehouse floor is open, with a 25-foot-high ceiling filled with rafters. Taking up only half of the building's upper floor, the second story contains an office and a loft that opens to the main warehouse floor for additional storage (with ropes and some swinging pulleys).

There is a wooden table in one corner of the ground floor where the cultists can eat, drink, and watch the entrances during the day. There's also a narrow stair along the wall closest to the cliff that leads down to a small storage room. The warehouse floor is filled with crates, barrels, and other containers fitting for a grain repository.

THE TRUE STORY

While the warehouse business pays the taxes, the cultists' true purpose is to spread chaos through Eldolan by summoning demons and releasing them into the town. To keep their activities secret, the cultists are using some caves in the cliffs next to the warehouse where they can perform their terrible rites unbothered. Thanks to the acquisitions of dead humanoid flesh they've made recently via Aerto, the summoning site has finally been prepared, and they are ready to call forth demons from the Abyss, bypassing the Great Gold Wyrm's wards. Now they only

SHADY PATRONS OF THE SQUIRMING MERMAID

When Scarlet calls for help against unruly PCs, run an improvised battle using one shady patron NPC for each PC in the group. (See NPC Stats section at the back of the adventure on page 66.) If the PCs push things, this should be a very difficult battle and there should be a good chance that the PCs will have to flee. If they're not the type to run and are defeated, you can choose to have the shady patrons toss the PCs into the bay down an extra recovery instead of having them be killed. Either way, don't count this battle as part of the group that gives a full heal-up. If the party is forced to flee, the campaign loss you choose could be that Aerto leaves during the commotion, never to be found, or something else that fits the story.

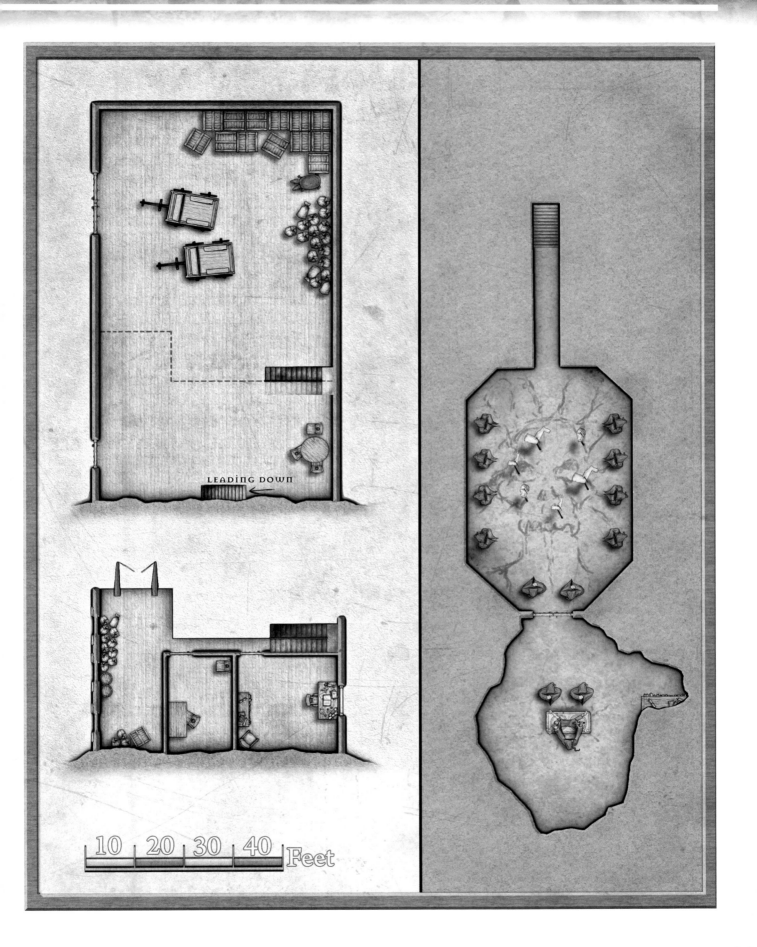

LEADING DOWN

10   20   30   40   Feet

need a living blood sacrifice to complete their ritual, but the PCs' arrival may disrupt their plans.

If any PCs have icon connections to the Diabolist, Crusader, Priestess, or the Great Gold Wyrm, there should be more story opportunities you can plant with these cultists.

ENTERING THE WAREHOUSE

The PCs arrive at the warehouse after darkness has fallen, watching it from an alley a block or two away. Lantern light glows dimly from the inside out through the narrow windows, and a torch burns in a sconce by the smaller door. Shortly after the PCs' arrival, they will spot a group of five humans (3 men, 2 women) wearing common laborer clothes approach the door, knock, and enter. As they wait, the PCs will hear one of the women giddily claim how excited she is that their wait is over and that the carnage shall soon begin, only to be hushed by an older man. The last cultist will take the torch from the front with him inside.

The group enters the building, bolts the door, descends down the stairs, dons robes, lights candles, and heads to the caves quickly. At that point, all of the cultists will be within the caverns, but the warehouse isn't unguarded.

Tactics: Assuming the PCs try to gain entrance to the place, they will need to bypass the bolt on the door (DC 15 to break it down or jimmy the bolt) or try to bypass the double wagon doors that have a large beam locking them from the inside (DC 20). If they fail the check, the PCs gain entrance but the noise alerts the guardian inside (no chance of surprising it). Alternately, a gnome or halfling PC could fit through one of the glassless high window openings if they climb to them (DC 15). No matter what method they use to get inside, the place will be mostly dark (one lantern turned low hangs by the stairs) and look empty. Hiding under the wagons on the warehouse floor is an **Abyssal guardian** that the cultists summoned. The guardian is the size of a donkey with an armored carapace and sports two horrific heads that are mostly jaws that emerge from the carapace to make attacks. It will stalk the PCs and attack, preferring to direct both heads toward one enemy to tear it to pieces.

FACING THE CULTISTS DURING THE DAY

The best time to face the cultists from an atmospheric perspective is during the night, but if the players won't go for it, things are a bit different at the warehouse and caves during the day. After their evening rituals, ten of the cultists return to their homes in the Commons until their shift starts in the afternoon. Four initiates and one elder in normal clothing will be working in the main building doing warehouse work. The Abyssal hound will be sleeping in the first cavern chamber, and Jeskill and four elders will be in the second chamber preparing it. Whether they made the sacrifice the night before and have the demon present or not is up to the GM.

If there are only 4 PCs, the guardian's *slavering double-bite* attack only deals 10 damage. If there are 6 PCs, add **three cult initiates** who were in one of the offices; they will investigate the sounds of battle and arrive in the second round.

ABYSSAL GUARDIAN

"Snap, snap!"

Double-strength 3ʳᵈ level wrecker [BEAST]
Initiative: +8

Slavering double-bite +8 vs. AC (2 attacks)—13 damage
Natural odd hit: The target also takes 5 ongoing acid damage.
Miss: 7 damage.

Invisibility: The first time the guardian is staggered during a battle, it becomes invisible until the end of its next turn or until it attacks. It gains a +2 bonus to its *slathering double bite* attack when it attacks while invisible.

Demonic senses: The guardian doesn't take a penalty to detect invisible creatures, or creatures using illusion to hide themselves.

AC	18	
PD	18	**HP 100**
MD	14	

CULT INITIATES (6 PCS ONLY)

"Flesh is weak!"

2ⁿᵈ level mook [HUMANOID]
Initiative: +5

Ritualistic blade +7 vs. AC—4 damage

Death is not the end: When a cult initiate drops to 0 hit points, each remaining member of the mob gains a +1 bonus to its attack until the end of its next turn (cumulative, max +4).

AC	17	
PD	12	**HP 9 (mook)**
MD	15	

Mook: Kill one cult initiate mook for every 9 damage you deal to the mob.

Loot: The guardian has nothing of value, though its body parts could be (demon ichor, etc.) There is a small iron strongbox kept in the second-floor office, however, which is used to make payments for deliveries. It holds 60 gp in silver and gold coins. If initiates are present, each has 1d4 gp.

Aftermath: The warehouse holds little of interest. The small basement storage room holds a few barrels of water with ladles and mugs, two boxes of candles on a large wood shelf, and pegs for 15 robes, with three still holding robes (if there were initiates in the building, or for three cultists not present). They are simple blood-red cloth robes with hoods.

There's a secret door in the room behind the wood shelf and finding and bypassing it requires a DC 25 Wisdom check. If they search (the room setup should make it obvious there must be a passage), the PCs will find the secret door no matter what the check result is, but if the first PC to search fails the check, they will also activate a strong ward in the tunnel beyond when they use the obvious catch to open the door instead of a better-hidden one.

ENTERING THE CAVES

If the PCs find and enter the caves during the day, adjust the descriptions of the chambers to account for the revised number of cultists outlined in the sidebar. Beyond the secret door, the passage goes from brick to natural stone as it enters the side of the cliff. A tunnel leads forty feet back to the first chamber of a two-part cavern. The cultists are currently performing a summoning ritual, intoning the Abyssal words in unison, with most of them in the first chamber and Jeskill and a few elders waiting in the second chamber to direct the summoning magic when the ritual words are completed.

Read to the players: *You see flickering light ahead of you accompanied by chanting and the smell of something foul. The tunnel ends at a long cavern whose outer edges angle upward slightly meeting the walls about 3 feet above the height of the central floor. Hanging from hooks on chains throughout the chamber are humanoid limbs, heads, and chunks of torsos; the body parts seem to be rotting away but are also coated with fresh blood. Designs drawn in blood and gore cover the floor in intricate patterns, and candles in polished blackened skulls burn from niches in the walls. At the far end of the cavern, a pair of iron double doors connects the chamber to another cavern. Ten red-robed and hooded figures are spread about the cavern chanting, and three more wait in the second cavern around a stone table upon which a bound man struggles to free himself. The ritual seems to be nearing completion as the cultists' voices grow louder.*

If the PCs failed the secret door check, as they approach the end of the tunnel and see the cavern and its inhabitants, a magical ward will activate. **Hard diabolic warding trap:** DC 20 to detect using Intelligence (if a PC is searching); **+10 vs. MD (each non-cultist in the tunnel)**—the target takes 5 ongoing psychic damage and hurls itself to the floor in the middle of the cavern as it is overcome by a strong mental compulsion. In addition, a deep, cold, unworldly voice intones, *"Bow before the true, non-believers!"* snapping the cultists out of their meditation. If the trap is not active and the PCs are stealthy, they may be able to surprise the cultists.

The first cavern is roughly 70 by 50 feet. There are eight cult initiates and two cult elders spread around it, and two more cult elders and the cult leader, Jeskill, waiting in the second cavern with their sacrificial victim. **Roll initiative!**

Tactics: Unless the PCs have used stealth or magic to sneak up on the cultists, the two elders with Jeskill will slam shut the iron doors at the end of the room and bar them before the first PC acts. Then all three will continue chanting the summoning ritual while their comrades in the first cavern defend the doors.

The **two cult elders** in the first chamber stand at the back of the cavern, in front of the iron doors, while the **eight cult initiates** stand around the raised outer edges of the room chanting. In this place, the cult elders have more power than usual. In addition to their normal attacks, they can use the Abyssal energy they've gathered to command the hooked chains in the ceiling to attack. Some of the cult initiates will move to the tunnel entrance to cut off escape, or to separate those inside from their allies, while the rest lunge in heartily with their blades seeking to further desecrate the chamber. They fight to the death with fanatical fervor.

The hooks descend from chains in the ceiling at different heights, with some as low as 3 feet from the ground. Creatures can climb them but they are slippery from gore and blood (a DC 15 Strength or Dexterity check to climb one and hang on each turn). It's also possible to counteract the magic in the chamber to make the hook attacks ineffective (see **aftermath**).

If there are only 4 PCs, remove two cult initiates. If there are 6 PCs, add a cult elder.

CULT INITIATES

"Flesh is weak!"

2nd level mook [HUMANOID]
Initiative: +5

Ritualistic blade +7 vs. AC—4 damage

Death is not the end: When a cult initiate drops to 0 hit points, each remaining member of the mob gains a +1 bonus to its attack until the end of its next turn (cumulative, max +4).

AC	17	
PD	12	HP 9 (mook)
MD	15	

Mook: Kill one cult initiate mook for every 9 damage you deal to the mob.

CULT ELDERS

"Can you hear her song?"

2nd level spoiler [HUMANOID]
Initiative: +5

Ritualistic scythe +7 vs. AC—6 damage
  Natural odd hit: The target also takes 5 ongoing damage.
  Miss: 2 ongoing damage.

C: Chains and hooks +7 vs. PD—5 damage, and the target is grabbed; when the target frees itself from the hook, it takes 3 damage
  Natural 16+: The target also takes 3 ongoing damage while grabbed by the hook.

Dedicated to the Diabolist: When a cult elder drops to 0 hit points, up to two cult initiates engaged with an enemy that was engaging the elder can make a melee attack against it as a free action.

AC	17	
PD	12	HP 32
MD	16	

Loot: There is little of value in the cavern or on the cultists, though searching them will reveal that they have all ritually scarred their bodies (in places clothes will hide) with the Diabolist's symbols. The rest of the cave's furnishings have no real value (to sane folk).

Aftermath: Chaotic energy is flowing from the first chamber to the second along the designs carved in the floor, which arcane or divine spellcasters who think to check might be able to detect (DC 15). If a PC succeeds in detecting the magic, they will also realize that it's possible to magically counteract some of the energy flow as a standard action (a DC 20 check, or you could allow a PC connected to the Diabolist, Crusader, or GGW the choice of making an icon relationship roll, with each 5 or 6 indicating some level of success). Doing so during the battle will negate the elders' *chains and hooks* ability until the start of that PC's next turn. Doing so after the battle will limit the effectiveness of the summoning ritual occurring in the second chamber. Whether before or after, each failure results in feedback damage, however, and the PC loses a recovery.

Unless the PCs somehow managed to get inside the second cavern (meaning a much harder battle including those inside as well but excluding the demon), allow them to take a quick rest after defeating the cultists in the first chamber without delaying their assault on the second chamber (a matter of seconds). Breaking through the iron doors requires three DC 20 Strength checks during battle, or about half a minute outside it (no checks

needed). If they were free to continue with the ritual, Jeskill and the elders will just be finishing their demon summoning as the PCs break the doors open.

DEALING WITH A DEMON

Assuming the cultists have been able to continue the ritual while their comrades fight off the PCs, they will be uttering the final intonations as the PCs break through the doors, otherwise they will join the battle in the first chamber. The **two cult elders** will intercept the PCs in the doorway while **Jeskill** tries to complete the ritual by sacrificing the sailor tied to a stone table in the center of the chamber.

Read to the players: *As you burst through the doors, the chanting stops. Two cultists step forward to intercept you as the third, a brown-bearded man in finer robes whose face is painted in blood says, "My lady, I call upon your power. Send us one of your children to slay these infidels!" You see the man, Jeskill from the description Aerto gave you, lift his blade. The man on the table renews his struggles, but the bonds hold.*

Tactics: The PCs have an opportunity to save the sailor (Jeffrys) if they are quick and lucky. He is on a table about twenty feet away from the doors. **Roll initiative!** Jeskill will go last in the round. On each of his turns, Jeskill will try to kill the sailor as he calls out to "Fargtu" to hear his call. At the start of his turn, he needs to be next to the sailor and will use all his actions to perform a coup de grace. If the sailor is helpless, Jeskill will kill the man without an attack roll. If this happens, the ritual magic will open a gate through the sailor's body and the demon **Fargtu** will emerge from the man's corpse, bloodily. Roll initiative for Fargtu and he can act on the next round.

If the PCs are thwarting Jeskill's attempts to summon the demon, Fargtu is willing to accept a different sacrifice to complete the ritual. When Jeskill is staggered, in a blaze of insanity he will drive his dagger into his chest and call the demon's name as a free action. Fargtu will accept the sacrifice of blood and emerge through Jeskill's now smoking corpse.

If the PCs have thwarted some of the chaotic energy of the ritual, Fargtu enters the battle weakened with 20% less hit points. There are also no hooked chains in the second cavern for the elders to use. If there are only 4 PCs, once Fargtu is summoned, Jeskill will rave at the PCs without attacking, or if he sacrificed himself, Fargtu will have 1 hp above his staggered value (28 or 23). If there are 6 PCs, add another cult elder.

Cult Elders

"Can you hear her song?"

2nd level spoiler [HUMANOID]
Initiative: +5

Ritualistic scythe +7 vs. AC—6 damage
Natural odd hit: The target also takes 5 ongoing damage.
Miss: 2 ongoing damage.

I will return: When a cult elder drops to 0 hit points, it can make a final *ritualistic scythe* attack as a free action.

AC	17	
PD	12	**HP 32**
MD	16	

Jeskill, Cult Leader

"Only the true will be rewarded."

3rd level leader [HUMANOID]
Initiative: Goes at end of round

Diabolic blade +8 vs. AC—8 damage
Natural 16+: The target also takes 5 damage of the following type of your choice: fire, cold, lightning, thunder.
Miss: Both Jeskill and the target take 1d4 damage.

Fervent words: Once per turn as a quick action, Jeskill can utter words of encouragement to one ally. That creature can make a melee attack as a free action and gains a +5 bonus to damage with that attack.

Protected by chaos: The first time each round Jeskill would take damage, chaotic energies reduce that damage by half.

AC	19	
PD	13	**HP 40**
MD	17	

Fargtu, Lesser Frenzy Demon

"I accept your sacrifice and answer your call."

4th level wrecker [DEMON]
Initiative: +8

Claw +8 vs. AC (2 attacks)—8 damage

Raging frenzy: Whenever Fargtu misses with a melee attack, it gains a +1 attack bonus and deals +1d4 damage until the end of the battle (maximum bonus +4, +4d4).

AC	20	
PD	16	**HP 55 (or 44)**
MD	15	

Loot: There is a box of black candles worth a few silvers, some blood collection bowls and urns carved from obsidian worth 50 gp if cleaned, and a small iron box covered with demonic designs. The box holds 140 gp, a ritual blade with a silver-forged grip set with a blood red ruby worth 150 gp, a **+1 Rune**, and a **+1 Holy Relic of Destruction**. *Always:* +1 attack and damage with a divine spell/attack; *Recharge 11+:* When you hit an enemy with an attack that deals holy damage, deal 1d10 extra holy damage with that attack. *Quirk:* Believes the world will come to a fiery end . . . soon.

Aftermath: In addition to the loot, there is also a bookshelf within a small alcove in the summoning chamber. It contains a handful of books on demon worship and summoning, as well as end-of-the-world stories about what will happen when the demon hordes are free to leave the Abyss. In addition, one thin book is Jeskill's journal. Besides his mad ravings about how the "true" will be graced to rule the world, and how his enemies will be treated when he's their lord, there is one relevant entry about Aerto.

Jeskill writes that one of his fellow cultists made contact with a black market dealer named Aerto. They watched the man and used divinations to determine he would suit their needs, even if his true allegiance was to a group of Lich King followers calling themselves "the Seekers of the Lost" who hide within the city in various organizations, including one member at the Dead Vaults. Jeskill believed Aerto could be trusted to provide for the cults' needs since he had his own secrets to hide, and so let him continue his charade.

This lead could send the PCs toward learning about Landon at the Dead Vaults, or to another lead if they've already pursued Landon (Sigmund and Paulos perhaps). If the group is ready for the next stage of their search, Jeskill's journal could mention the Lamplighters and Arlissa Thent specifically.

ROLLO THE THIN, TEMPLE DISTRICT

A halfling tent vendor named Rollo the Thin recognized one of the zombies as a deceased friend who had been laid to rest.

TALKING TO ROLLO THE THIN

Rollo is easy enough to find; he's in Hawker's Square at his tent selling pipes and tobacco from the Twisp region. Rollo's naming is obvious when the PCs first meet him, because he's exceptionally tall and lean for a halfling. He sports a pencil-thin mustache and sandy-blonde hair, and looks to have some gnome blood in his line. Rollo talks quick and becomes easily distracted by potential customers passing by who might want his wares, to the point that he will ignore the PCs or forget their questions, unless of course they are also buying something from him! He will return to his booth shortly after the attack to make sure no one runs off with his goods, and is there each day during daylight hours.

When asked about the zombie attack, Rollo will be forthcoming, saying that one of the zombies was definitely his friend Koln, a human bricklayer he'd known for years. Poor Koln was trampled by a runaway horse just a week ago. His family paid for his burial at the town crypts, which are known as the Dead Vaults, and Rollo went to the service and everything. So imagine his surprise when he saw big Koln rampaging through the square, with his chest cut open revealing his missing heart and lungs.

Rollo will say, *"How can someone laid to rest all proper-like at the crypts get made into one of them undead zombie things? It just don't make sense."* And he's right, normally that can't happen if the proper burial rituals are performed. But someone at the Dead Vaults has been tampering with the recently deceased. This information should make the PCs want to visit the Dead Vaults in the Temple district, since Rollo is right: the magical point of proper burials is to prevent zombie rampages.

THE TEMPLE DISTRICT

Although it isn't a large section of town, magic-centric Eldolan does have a Temple district. It houses many small shrines and a few larger temples to the Gods of Light (or whichever pantheon you're using), offering services to those who seek divine guidance and housing numerous clerics and church officials, many of whom work for the Priestess. It's also the site for the Dead Vaults.

The district is located along the southeastern edge of the town next to the Commons and down the cliffs from the Grounds above. The crypts of the Dead Vaults are housed under a stone temple that acknowledges all of the Gods of Light by displaying statues of each around its perimeter. The temple is simple, but the crypts underneath it extend downward and outward far further than most realize.

If the heroes are seeking any sort of divine help, the Temple district (called Temples by the locals) is the place to go. Many of the priests and priestesses there are willing to perform rituals for hefty donations to the Priestess' coffers, and/or their particular church. There are also plenty of self-proclaimed oracles (some might even be so) who linger around the periphery of the district selling religious trinkets and charms. Lamplighter lanterns shine brightly throughout the small district at night, and each temple has commissioned its own lanterns, crafted with the deity's motifs of course. The Silver Shields patrol the district regularly.

ICON INVOLVEMENTS IN TEMPLES

Recently, a group of the Crusader's dark clerics arrived in town following rumors of groups of raiders dedicated to the Orc Lord consorting with demons in the lands east of town. These priests have been flaunting their dark gods to the other clergy in the district and trying to gain new followers from the faithful of the Gods of Light. The priests have come into conflict with an order of paladins dedicated to the Great Gold Wyrm currently in town. They're also beginning to annoy those who work for the Priestess in the district with their constant rebuttals of the weakness of that icon.

Any PC with ties to the Great Gold Wyrm, Priestess, or Crusader might get pulled into the religious infighting while in Temples. And any PC with connections to the Orc Lord might run afoul of the dark clerics and their accusations as well.

THE DEAD VAULTS

The vaults are not open to the public, except during times of burial, and then only to friends and family in the burial-ritual chambers. A small group of priests led by **Odessa Rilantes**, a human cleric of the Gods of Light who serves the Priestess, maintains the crypts and performs burial rituals for the recently deceased (for a "donation"). Mourners are allowed into the temple above and also in the chambers where the rituals of burial are performed. The influential or wealthy without their own mausoleums often have arrangements so they and their kin are buried in the same section of the crypts, and these folk can also gain direct access to those crypts if the need arises. Odessa will swear that Rollo's story is false, and believes it, but that's not the truth.

THE TRUE STORY

As far as Odessa knows, she is correct about the deceased receiving the proper burial rituals. The problem, of course, is that one of Odessa's acolytes, a human priest named Landon Smithson, actually serves the Seekers of the Lost and has been faking the rituals and desecrating the crypts. He is careful not to do it very often, and performs the subterfuge only on the more common folk whose families can barely afford the donation (since those who are too poor to pay have only one choice: cremation), so that none will come to pay respects and notice the broken seals on their loved-one's crypt. So far his actions have remained unnoticed, but the heroes' arrival may change things.

TALKING TO ODESSA

If the PCs show up wanting to learn more about the Dead Vaults, asking questions about whether the bodies are correctly interned there, start snooping about, or are actually making claims about how the zombies from Hawker's Square were from the crypts, the lesser priests will quickly summon Odessa. This lead is as much about getting her to work with the heroes as it is dealing with Landon. She will ask the PCs what they want, or if they have made accusations, ask them for proof of such "outrageous claims." If the PCs have only Rollo's word, she will be offended, stating that she and her people always perform the proper rituals to ensure that the dead are set to rest. She is adamant that the crypts have not been disturbed and that such accusations are unwarranted (even if it's not a direct accusation).

Odessa is a small, middle-aged woman with graying blonde hair pulled back into a tight ponytail. She wears formal robes and vestments of a cleric of the Gods of Light, adorned also with the symbol of the Priestess. She speaks in short, clipped sentences and tends to sniff hard after ending each one. She smiles rarely, takes her duty very seriously, and is used to people obeying her. The acolytes scurry at her slightest glance.

Odessa will quickly try to put any concerns by the PCs to rest, and will be insulted at the thought of her people failing their duty, so she will ask the PCs to leave. At this point, the PCs can attempt to smooth things over with her to have an actual discussion. It will take at least one DC 15 Charisma check (using diplomacy or bluffing) to appease her, and perhaps more checks depending on how the heroes approach the interaction. If there is a PC with relationship points with the Priestess in the group, that PC gains a +2 bonus to any checks, or +4 if they are also a cleric. If a PC wants to use their icon relationships in this situation, any PCs

that have a positive or conflicted relationship with the Priestess or negative relationship with the Lich King can roll their relationship dice for those icons. Any advantages gained can be used to get Odessa to talk (she hopes to one day be invited to work at the Cathedral and won't pass on a chance to hobnob with someone who's "connected"). Any 5s will create complications with that icon as normal; one possibility in exchange for her help is that Odessa will require a PC to promise to put their support behind her and to take a letter of introduction to the Priestess' people at the Cathedral with suggestions that she be given a post there.

Getting Odessa to actually agree to let the PCs enter the crypts will require a second successful DC 15 Charisma skill check or icon dice advantage. If the PCs fail the checks and are unable to use their connections, they still have a means of getting access. During the discussion one of Odessa's acolytes (Thomas) will interrupt at some point. He will relate how he found a few of the crypt seals broken a few weeks ago in the commons wing (where the common folk are buried), and some odd stains on the stone floor. Odessa will hush him, but the information will be enough to make her change her mind so that the PCs will be satisfied and leave (fail forward!). If it takes Thomas' interjection to get Odessa to let them see the crypts, however, the battle to come will be more difficult (see tactics).

This is also a good opportunity for PCs with Priestess relationships to pick up additional information for side quests and stories that relate to the icon or to their *uniques*.

ENTERING THE CRYPTS

Once Odessa decides to allow the PCs to see the crypts (probably to visit Koln's crypt, the zombie who Rollo recognized), she will assign Thomas to escort them to the Dead Vaults, though she will warn them to show proper respect or they'll have to answer to the Mage Council. Thomas looks to be about twenty five, with a smooth-skinned face, shaved pate, and short brown hair around the sides. He bears the symbol of the Priestess on a silver disc hanging from a beaded chain around his neck. He also is starved for conversation, especially about any news from the world outside of Eldolan.

Thomas will lead the PCs down a set of stairs, past various burial chambers, and into the crypts, following a charting system that lists the name of each person entombed there. There are many passages leading to different sections, creating a bit of a maze of tunnels. He carries a lantern and will lead them first to the area for the common folk (like Koln), assuming that's where the PCs want to go. That section of the vaults is larger than the rest, with many narrow parallel corridors filled floor to ceiling with crypts just big enough to entomb a body and sealed with brick and mortar. Each one also has warding symbols inscribed upon the outer bricks as an added precaution against the Lich King's call, though such wards are physically very faded on many of the oldest crypts.

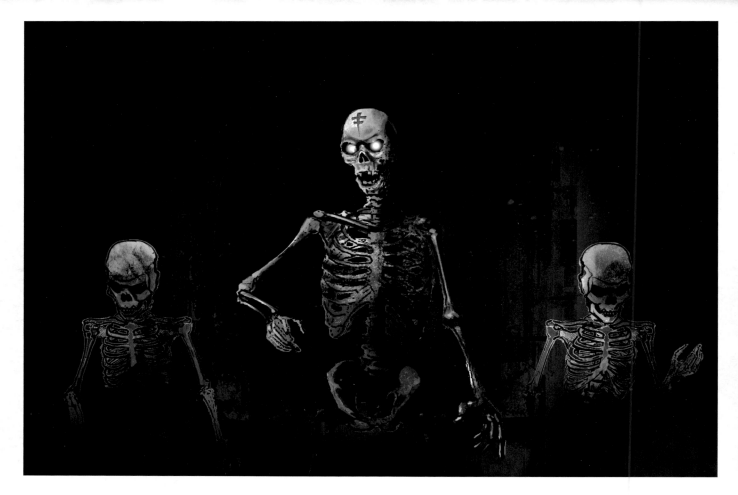

When they arrive at Koln's crypt, one thing will become obvious with minimal searching: the warding symbols have been scraped off and the bricks are stacked but not mortared. Removing the bricks will reveal no body within. Thomas will be highly agitated by this, and when questioned about it, he will say that he must find Landon, the acolyte in charge of this area, to determine how it could have happened.

LANDON'S STORY

Landon Smithson is a member of the Seekers. He will also be present (in a corner) along with a handful of other acolytes when the PCs arrive at the Dead Vaults to talk to Odessa. If they talk Odessa into letting them enter the crypts, Landon realizes that a careful examination will reveal the truth of it, and the fact that he is the one in charge of the areas that have been desecrated. Knowing this, he will enter the crypts ahead of them. Once the PCs reach Koln's crypt (or are searching that general area) and the truth is revealed, Landon will decide that his time as an acolyte is done and enact a ritual he has spent months putting into place.

He has desecrated many of the older crypts in the area and removed the wards, allowing the Lich King's call to reach them. Garados taught him a ritual to raise the bodies as undead, and he has been working on it for months. There were plans to raise a much larger horde in the future, but now Landon only wishes to kill the heroes if possible, and escape to report to Garados.

Once he sets the undead skeletons upon the PCs, he will flee via a secret tunnel from the Dead Vaults to the Seeker's hidden sanctum to report.

SKELETON ATTACK

When Thomas gives Landon's name to the PCs as the acolyte in charge of the area, Landon will call out in a high-pitched boy-like voice from his hiding spot out of sight to taunt Thomas and the PCs, saying: *Fools! Always thinking you were so safe, and that your Priestess and her rituals would protect you. Well, the One-eyed Lord will have his day, and then you and your kind will bow before us. Well, not you. It's your time to die!* He will then yell out a few words of power to activate his ritual and shout a command to the undead to kill everyone. Then the PCs will hear receding footfalls. Thomas will curse Landon out loud, recognizing his voice.

Read to the players: *As the man's voice chants out the last syllable you hear what sounds like a deep, rasping exhalation come from all around you, followed by the disturbing sounds of bricks hitting stone. At the edge of the lantern's light, you see a thin, skeletal figure with creaking sinews push its way out of a crypt. More of its kind quickly join it, some with a bluish-purple light emanating from their hollow eye slots. Two separate groups move toward you, one each toward the two open archways into the chamber. Thomas screams!*

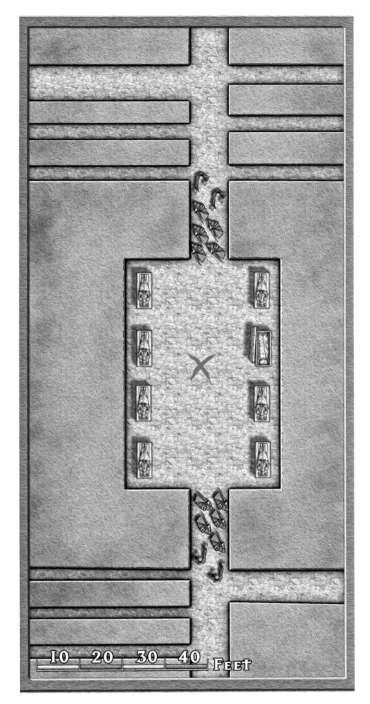

Tactics: Landon has animated 14 skeletons: **4 skeleton mages** and **10 dead vault skeletons** (two mobs of 5). This is a double-strength battle. The PCs are currently in a 30 by 60 foot crypt chamber with a corridor exiting it from each end through a 10-foot-wide archway, with many smaller corridors branching off those corridors beyond the chamber (see map above). The skeletons will approach from both exits and won't stop attacking until destroyed. Two skeletal mages will stay behind each mob, attacking at range with blasts of magic force from their eyes. Once at least two skeletons in the mob in front of them are down, one of the mages will use *call of the grave* to try to revive them. Until they are staggered, the mages are also willing to take opportunity attacks to use their ranged attack if they aren't able to disengage. **Roll initiative!**

Thomas will try to hide in a corner (he is more of a functionary who can perform basic rituals than a true divine caster), but one or two of the dead vault skeletons will attack him if they can reach him and he will try to disengage and call for help (**AC** 12; **PD** 11; **MD** 11 **HP** 15). If the PCs set up a strong defense at both exits, roll a save at the start of each round to see if Thomas bolts past them for the exit when there's an opening; on a failure, he tries to flee and gets trapped by any remaining skeletons in the corridor he chose. If the party doesn't have a cleric, consider holding a skeleton mage and a few mooks back in a second wave that enters the battle when the escalation die reaches 2.

This part of the crypt has been desecrated by Landon, tilting things in favor of the undead. Each time the escalation die would increase, have one of the PCs roll an easy save (6+). On a failure, the escalation die doesn't increase that round. As a move action, any PC with an appropriate background, or that has relationship points with the Priestess or Lich King, can attempt to offset the unholy energy by rolling a DC 15 Wisdom check. A success means no saving throw is required next turn to see if the escalation die increases.

If there are only 4 PCs, remove one skeleton mage and two dead vault skeletons. If there are 6 PCs, add one skeleton mage and two dead vault skeletons. If the PCs required Thomas' help to gain access to the crypts (by failing checks), the skeletal mages aren't vulnerable to holy damage due to Landon's desecration of the area. Allow anyone wielding a bashing weapon like a hammer, mace, or staff to ignore the skeletons' *resist weapons* ability, if you wish.

DEAD VAULT SKELETONS

"Ahhhhhhhhhh."

1st level mook [UNDEAD]
Initiative: +6
Vulnerability: holy

Skeletal claw +6 vs. AC—3 damage

Resist weapons 16+: When a weapon attack targets this creature, the attacker must roll a natural 16+ on the attack roll or it only deals half damage.

Speed of the dead: Due to the ritual magic used to create it, the mob this skeleton belongs to can roll two d20 for initiative and take the best result.

AC	16	
PD	14	**HP 6 (mook)**
MD	11	

Mook: Kill one decrepit skeleton mook for every 6 damage you deal to the mob.

SKELETON MAGE

"You disssturb our resssst."

2ⁿᵈ level caster [UNDEAD]
Initiative: +7
Vulnerability: holy

Bony rake +6 vs. AC—4 damage

R: Bluefire rays +6 vs. PD (up to 2 nearby enemies in a group)—4 force damage
Natural even hit: The target is vulnerable until the start of the mage's next turn.

Call of the grave: Once per battle as a quick action, the skeleton mage can roll a normal save to bring slain mook allies back to unlife. On a success, 1d2 dead vault skeletons rejoin the battle at the start of that mob's turn (add their hit points to the mob's total; they aren't viable targets before that time).

Resist weapons 16+: When a weapon attack targets this creature, the attacker must roll a natural 16+ on the attack roll or it only deals half damage.

AC	17	
PD	12	**HP 30**
MD	16	

Loot: The dead vault skeletons have nothing of value on them. The skeletal mages were once wizards, and each was buried with 1d6 x 10 gp in jewelry on them (though Thomas will object weakly to anyone looting the dead).

Aftermath: Once the PCs defeat the undead horde, Odessa and the other priests will arrive to find out what all of the noise was about. If Thomas is alive, he will tell her what happened and describe Landon's treachery (he recognized his voice). They will realize that their group was infiltrated. If Thomas didn't survive, the heroes might have to do more explaining, though the skeletal bodies everywhere and a few divinations by the priests should reveal the truth of things to them without too much trouble other than taking time.

Following Landon quickly doesn't seem to be an option: Landon used a secret exit to escape the vaults and never passed through the upper temple. Finding the entrance among so many crypts and passages would take days, or magic that is more powerful than what the PCs have at hand.

A search of Landon's cell will reveal a few things. First, there's a sheet of paper next to his simple bed with the Lamplighter's Guild schedule of lighting duties for their wizards in the Saddle for the past week. There's also a small shelf of prayer books, and among them is a much darker tome that discusses the power a divine caster can accumulate through raising and controlling the residual lifeforce (or animus) of deceased humanoids. It's incriminating evidence that Landon actually served the Lich King's purposes. In addition, there's a folded note in the back of the book. It says:

Your efforts are appreciated Landon, especially with our lord's most recent request. His power grows stronger with every passing week. Although I realize your stock might be running low, my work is coming to a crucial point and I need more freshly dead bodies. Hopefully the attack will provide those. Seek out Paulos at the Dreammaster's in the Commons for further instructions.

This final piece of incriminating evidence is all Odessa needs to believe Landon was a spy and foe of the Priestess. It may also lead the heroes to the Dreammaster (and Paulos and Sigmund) in the Commons, or if they've already pursued that lead, drop a clue to one of the other leads. If the group is ready for the next stage of their search, you could have the note instruct Landon to seek out Arlissa Thent instead.

Additional loot: In thanks for their help in rooting out the traitor among them, Odessa will offer the PCs some aid in their search and for possible future battles. She gives them two **Potions of Healing** (adv tier), a small stoppered vial of **Divine Tears of Halnir** (see Magical Aid), and a **Charm of Negative Energy Resistance** (a one-use item that will crumble afterward; small clay medallion with Priestess' symbol on it; activate it with a quick action to gain *resist negative energy 16+* for one battle or five minutes).

RUMNEY'S FRIEND, THE SADDLE

A Hawker's Square vendor named Rumney knows who owns the pumpkin cart in the square that was blocking the road. The owner might be connected to the attack.

TALKING TO RUMNEY

Rumney Twosilvers is a dwarven craftsman who sells his fine stone sculptures in Eldolan's markets. He owns a small shop in the Saddle where he makes his works of art. The day of the zombie attack, he set up a table facing the road entrance where the pumpkin cart was located. He was paying attention to the cart because it was blocking traffic, and he was mad about the loss of customers passing his booth.

Rumney has a thick accent, a dark black beard braided with green stone beads, and a bald pate. His hands are so rough and calloused they look like they are made from stone. He isn't the type to be loose with his tongue, knowing that words spoken to the wrong folk can be dangerous, but he is sociable. He's extra sociable, however, to those who buy one (or more) of his carvings (starting at 3 gp). Once the PCs get him talking, if asked what he knows about the cart, its owner, the accident, or the attack, he can relate the following:

- A pair of robed men drove the cart to the square; he couldn't see their faces because they wore their hoods for some reason. Their robes looked like those the wizard students wear, though. (If pressed, he will say he thinks they were grayish-silver not mithril colored, but he will seem unsure about that fact—don't give the PCs too strong a case to confront Mithril.)
- The men purposely stopped their mule right at the entrance to the square, fully blocking the way. (Rumney was mad about that.) Then one of them unhitched the cart and tipped it backward, spilling the pumpkins. (Rumney was confused by that.)
- The two robed fellows (he's very sure they were human men) then quickly made for the main exit, leaving their cart and pumpkins behind. That's when the zombie attacked the Silver Shield guard and the undead hordes rushed into the square. Then that pumpkin chucker rose out of the cart and started pummeling folks with squash.
- Rumney didn't recognize the robed fellows, but he did recognize the pumpkin cart, and specifically the mule, as those belonging to a half-elven merchant named Pazarius Rane who owns a small stables and general store near Rumney's shop in the Saddle. The mule definitely belonged to Pazarius, because it bit Rumney one time as he was passing by, though Rumney is unsure about the pumpkins.

THE SADDLE

The Saddle rests between the Grounds and the Governs on their hills to the east and west, and the Docks and Commons to the north and south. It's the home of craftsfolk and merchants of all stripes, some who have a touch of magical talent they infuse into their work. The Saddle's streets are wider and more organized, the Silver Shields patrol the district regularly (though now less often during the evening hours), and it's well-lit by the Lamplighter's Guild lanterns at night. It's the center of Eldolan.

There is also a lot of business that goes on after-hours among the many merchants, minor nobles, and wizard students who regularly roam among the district's many taverns, beer halls, and performance houses. Workshops range from single-dwelling structures to large, multi-story affairs teeming with masters and apprentices. Getting into the Saddle gates usually costs a few coppers, so poor folk without the coin or a worknote from a business or crafthouse giving them passage rarely get past the guards.

The Saddle is the location of one of the primary Lamplighter's Guild offices, a structure called the Lanternwerks near the more sparse northeastern edge of the district. It also houses the Waterworks, a large stone building with only two floors aboveground but many stories below built around the river—Uller's Flow—that travels through the district underground. The Waterworks magically supplies fresh water to each district, including high up to the Grounds and the Governs, and is run by the Krielson dwarven clan (but not outlined in this adventure).

ICON INVOLVEMENTS IN THE SADDLE

The Saddle houses many with skill in crafting and talent with magic, allowing them to create potions, oils, and other magical or semi-magical items for purchase. Many of the craftsfolk are dwarven, or have ties to the Dwarf King. They also pay well for special components gathered in the wilds and from the far ends of the Empire, often doing business with those who have connections to the High Druid to gain access to such places.

Recently, Imperial troops fighting skirmishes against the warriors and barbarians flying the Orc Lord's banner have had to deal with a troublesome issue. The Orc Lord's folk have been using alchemical items during their attacks: poison gas, acid, exploding fire, and worse. Agents of the Emperor have tracked the items and determined that they're being created in Eldolan, and most likely in the Saddle. PCs with connections to any of those icons might be approached to help ferret out those responsible, or to help smuggle the goods out of the town. (For that matter, PCs with ties to the Prince might come into play for that as well.)

TALKING TO PAZARIUS

Pazarius Rane is a half-elven merchant with a slick tongue who deals in all types of goods, most of them legal. He has dark hair with bright blue eyes, but sports an old scar on his right cheek that makes him look a little dangerous. He owns a general store but does most of his business hiring out wagons and mules from his small stables for construction projects in town. Within a few hours of the attack at Hawker's Square, Pazarius will have heard about the cart of pumpkins that was blocking the road; he knows it was a cart and mule that he sold, and he's scared that the fallout will come back on him. That's why he didn't come forward or say anything after the attack. Association with that type of event will kill his business.

For four days after the attack, he keeps the shop doors and windows locked to show that the business is closed and he won't go outside. If the PCs knock persistently, or make threats or bribes, he'll eventually open an upstairs window and ask the heroes what they want. Some basic surveillance will also reveal that someone is in the shop and apartments above it (as will questioning the local street urchins at the cost of a few coppers).

Getting Pazarius to reveal anything about the cart won't be easy, requiring a successful DC 15 Charisma check (diplomacy, bluff), Strength check (intimidation), or similar check using a different method. Mentioning that his cart and mule was identified by someone at the square might also be enough for him to try to do damage control. Even if the PCs fail their checks, to fail forward you should have the half-elf eventually open up

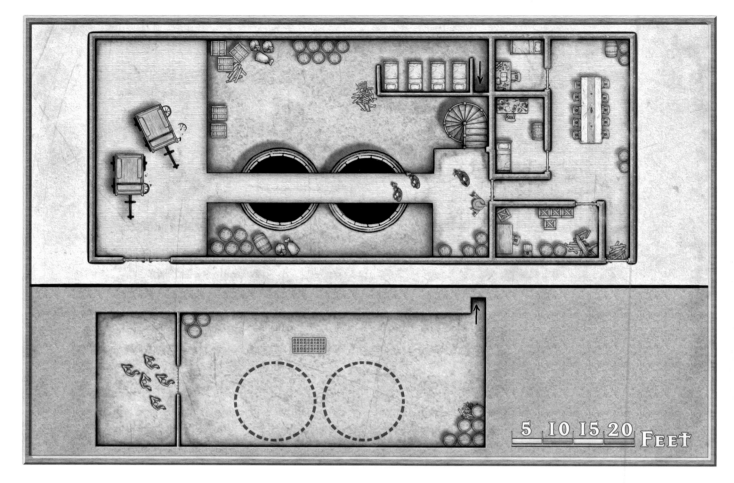

to the PCs, but the price of failure is that Grayson has spies watching the place who report the PCs' interest, allowing him to be more prepared.

One way or another, once the PCs get Pazarius talking, he will relate the following information:

- The cart and mule belonged to him. A farmer traded the pumpkins for some equipment, and Pazarius was looking for a vendor who would buy them.
- The day before the attack, a man came into the shop and made Pazarius an offer to buy the mule, cart, and pumpkins that he couldn't resist (35 gp). The price seemed overly high, and he wondered on it a bit, but at that price he didn't ask any questions.
- The man, a human who called himself Grayson, wore the clothes of a laborer, but his hands weren't calloused and he didn't have the look of a working man. Pazarius noticed that Grayson had a brass chain around his neck in the style that seemed familiar, but he's not sure where from. (It's similar to those the Lamplighter's Guild wizards wear as a symbol of their guild; if a PC tries to help him recall that detail somehow, like with hypnotism or magic, allow them a DC 25 check to do so.)
- As Grayson was leaving, Pazarius overheard the man tell someone waiting outside (he didn't see the person) that they would store the cart at the "Old Brewery." He thought it a bit odd because everyone knows that the Old Brewery is vacant and haunted.
- He will ask the PCs who they're with and plead (whining at times) with them not to mention his involvement in any of the mess.

Based on the info, the Old Brewery is probably the PCs' next stop, though if the PCs managed to learn of the Lamplighter connection, perhaps they will travel to the Lanternwerks. Of course, Grayson is an alias and no one by that name works at the guild. Anyone in the Saddle can point out the location of the brewery.

☦HE OLD BREWERY

Located near the wall separating the Saddle from the Docks, the Old Brewery was once the primary distillery and ale-making site for a group of dwarves in town known as the Alemasters. It suited the dwarves' purposes early in the town's history, but demand for their fine ales (including their *Hammerblow stout*) and strong liquors quickly outpaced what the brewery could produce. That fact, coupled with a few accidents stemming from excessive drunkenness among the workers and construction choices made for easy distribution of the product and not worker safety, soon forced the Alemasters to build a much larger and safer brewery in the Commons. The old brewery continued to be used for experimental brews, but after another handful of accidents, it was finally closed down completely.

It remained that way for many years, gaining a reputation for being haunted by all the former workers who had died there. These rumors continued thanks to various vagrants and homeless folk who lived in the place over the years being seen moving about the place at night. Seeing an opportunity, the Seekers moved into the building a few years back, clearing out the riffraff and maintaining the place as a storage facility and sometimes meeting location. The occasional faked spirit sighting, or well-placed knife in the back, has kept both citizens and vagabonds away from the Old Brewery ever since.

Grayson (real named Abrose Fuller) and his people recently used the place to store the cart used in the attack at Hawker's Square. They've also prepared the place against unwanted visitors. His helper, Jalen, was the one who thought it would be fun to put a zombie in the pumpkin cart, with the last-minute addition of a carved pumpkin head on it for added impact (and laughs for him).

THE OLD BREWERY LAYOUT

Grayson is not alone at the Old Brewery. His assistant, a twenty-year-old human man named Jalen, works with him on most endeavors. Jalen isn't fully aware of Grayson's connection with the Seekers of the Lost, but he knows Grayson deals with bad people and he's fine with it as long as Grayson keeps paying well. Both are hiding out at the brewery after the attack, waiting for things to cool down. Given time, one or the other will emerge to get supplies, but that won't happen until at least three or four days after the attack.

The Old Brewery consists of three main areas: the brew room, the offices and drinking hall, and the storage chambers below the brew room. See map opposite for more details.

BREW ROOM

The brew room takes up more than half the building and spans two floors. A pair of heavy wooden doors meant for wagons allows access to the brew room from the street outside, but they are locked on the inside with a heavy chain and padlock. The doors slide open just enough to give access to the padlock.

Examination will reveal that the padlock is oiled and has seen recent use. Breaking the chain or picking the lock requires a DC 15 check. Failure means the PCs bypass the lock or door, but make a lot of noise doing so (if they were trying to be quiet) and Grayson and Jalen hear them, allowing them to surprise the PCs once they move inside.

Inside the doors is a small landing where two broken wagons lie collapsed. To their right, a set of pulleys and winches attached to thick ceiling beams fifteen feet overhead trail tattered ropes down into a recessed pit that takes up most of the rest of the brew room. At the bottom of the 30-foot pit are two huge wooden vats set side by side (the vat walls are 15-feet high). A wooden walkway without rails crosses directly over the top of the vats to another landing on the other side of the room 40 feet away. From the landing, a door enters into the offices and drinking hall on the ground level, and a rickety set of stairs circles down to the bottom of the pit by the vats. A window in one of the offices looks out over the brew room.

In addition to the vats on the bottom level of the brew room, there are work tables, empty kegs, various copper pipes leading all over, and an archway leading to a small separate bunk area for workers to sleep (or sleep one off). In addition, there's a narrow ramp (out of sight from above) that leads from the bunk room down to the storage chambers below the pit.

OFFICES AND DRINKING HALL

On the ground floor, there is a normal-sized door from the outside into the drinking hall (the old worker entrance), but it has been boarded up inside and out and will require time (and make a lot of noise) to open. The small drinking hall has a large wooden table with a few empty kegs set up around it as makeshift chairs. There's a short corridor to a door to the brewery, and three offices that open back onto the hall. One of the offices also has a window overlooking the brew room. Grayson and Jalen have turned two of the offices into sleeping quarters, and the third into a storeroom for food and drink.

HAVING SOME GHOSTLY FUN

At any point once the PCs enter the brewery, but especially as the battle with Grayson ramps up, you could add a humorous element to the action in the form of a dwarven spirit of a former brewery worker who died on the job, Welgar Drabspar. Welgar haunts the brewery, unaware of the fact that he's dead. He originally died on the job, falling into the pit and breaking his neck while dead drunk. His spirit is cursed to remain in the brewery in a drunken state until he realizes (or someone finds a way to inform him through his drunken haze) that he's dead.

When Welgar appears, he will stumble about between combatants, berate people for damaging the place, lecture people to be careful on the walkway ("the boss gets mad when people get hurt"), and generally play the confused drunk taking on the role of battle commenter. As a spirit, he can't be harmed.

Alternately, if you want him to have an impact on the battle, you could give him a limited ability to affect the living. As a standard action, a PC can attempt to convince the spirit to help them by making a DC 20 skill check. Success means the dwarf spirit confronts an opponent, pushing them off balance or holding them in place (stuck until the end of their next turn). Failure means the dwarf turns on the PC and does the same to them.

If you use Welgar, once the battle is over, he could be a source of information about the brewery (perhaps there's a secret stash hidden somewhere, including one magic item if the group didn't get much magical aid from the icons at the start) or provide other useful information about the town from ten years ago if the PCs can convince him to help. Or perhaps the PCs could help him find his final rest and receive a boon of some sort for doing so.

STORAGE CHAMBERS

There are two rooms in a cellar directly below the brew room, connected by a narrow ramp that leads back to the brew room. The chambers were used for overflow tanks, a small hand pump, and storage of yeast and other ale-making materials, as well as the spent mash. Although the mash pile rotted away long ago, the place still smells of it. There are two circular holes in the ceiling directly below each vat with short copper pipes attached to them; obviously once part of a drainage system. A large grate covers a drain in the floor that connects to the town sewers.

Grayson has converted the second chamber into a cell, where he keeps his pets, a small pack of ghouls.

ENTERING THE BREWERY

Grayson and Jalen are currently laying low in the brewery, drinking and gambling in the hall to pass the time. Anyone trying to get in through the boarded-up door will give them plenty of warning, and they will move into the brew room on the opposite side of the walkway to prepare an ambush from behind the cart wreckage. Grayson also keeps a pair of dwarf skeletons in the storage room as extra protection.

If the PCs enter through the large brew room doors, picking the lock or breaking the chain, the noise might alert Grayson as well, but there is also a secondary alarm system. As soon as any PC steps into the room, a small watch-sprite that looks like a skeletal goblin will suddenly pop into existence in front of them and ask in a shrill voice, "What's the word?"

The "word" is *ghostface* (Jalen's joke), but the PCs are unlikely to know it (though an icon advantage works great here). If they fail to give the password immediately or give the wrong password, the sprite will begin to scream, alerting Grayson. If a quick-thinking PC wants to either magically dismiss the sprite or confuse it somehow, you could allow it but it would be difficult, requiring the character to succeed at a DC 25 check. Adjust the following text if the PCs find a way to appease the sprite, or if they make too much noise getting inside (in which case Grayson dismisses the sprite while waiting in ambush), or if they enter from the dining hall. **Roll initiative!**

Read to the players: *As the small sprite screams, you get a better look at the inside of the brewery. You're on a landing near a rectangular pit that drops some thirty feet. A pair of large, empty wooden vats stand side by side sit at the bottom of the pit and their walls rise perhaps halfway up it. A narrow wooden walkway crosses over the vats to another landing about forty feet away on the far side of the room. There's a rickety set of circular stairs on that side going down, and a door leading into the rest of the building on the main floor. The door suddenly opens and two short, thick skeletons enter and move to the walkway, followed by a pair of humans, one wearing robes. The skeletons were surely dwarves at one time. The robe wearer sneers at you and says, "You shouldn't have come here fools. You'll die for it!"*

Tactics: The **two dwarf skeletons** will move to guard the walkway at Grayson's order. **Jalen**, who has a crossbow, and **Grayson** (Ambrose), who is actually a wizard of some skill, will remain on the landing behind them using ranged attacks. (Each will make a ranged attack before the first round if they surprise the PCs; and they will be on the opposite side of the brew room if the PCs force their way through the boarded-up door.) Grayson has two tricks up his sleeve, however. He has placed an explosive rune upon the walkway near its center. As a free action, he can utter a word and ignite the rune, bringing the bridge down and sending anyone on it plummeting into the pit below. He'll wait to use the rune until at least one PC has safely crossed the walkway, targeting the second to come across (leaving the first PC—with only a few feet of broken walkway behind them—to deal with the two skeletons). Note, if you have a dwarf skeleton move to intercept the first PC crossing the walkway, you could choose to have both that PC and skeleton potentially fall into the pit when the second PC tries to cross, letting each roll a normal save to avoid falling.

Any other PCs on the walkway farther than 5 feet from the edge might also fall into the pit/vat. Those near the edges who succeed at a normal save will fall to the pit floor and not into a vat. In either case, anyone who falls will take 3d6 damage. The problem, however, is that the bottoms of the vats have rotted out over the years. Those falling in will keep going through to the floor of the storage chamber another 15 feet down (no extra damage thanks to the softened landing of rotten wood). The walkway will have a 30-foot gap in the middle of it (a DC 20 check to jump with a running start).

That's where Grayson's second trick comes into play. He keeps a pack of **five newly-risen ghouls** trapped behind bars in the second storage chamber below. As a quick action, he can release the magical ward that holds the barred door to the ghouls' cell closed, allowing them to pour out and attack, and they are very hungry! Moving from the cellar up the ramp to the brewery room floor takes a full round, but any PCs on the edge of the pit looking down into the room below the vats can consider allies there nearby.

If there are only 4 PCs, remove a ghoul and dwarf skeleton. If there are 6 PCs, add three ghouls. If Grayson's people were watching Pazarius Rane, Grayson and his allies will automatically surprise the heroes since they'll be waiting for them. If the PCs find a way to surprise Grayson, the walkway/vats might not come into play, but Grayson will still release the ghouls to cause a distraction. In that case, they will emerge from the storage chamber and enter the battle when the escalation die is at 2. If at least two PCs fall through the vats into the cellar, this becomes a double-strength battle.

NEWLY-RISEN GHOUL

"We hungersssss."

2nd level mook [UNDEAD]
Initiative: +5
Vulnerability: holy

Scrabbling claws +7 vs. AC—3 damage
 Natural 16+ The target is vulnerable (*attacks vs. it have crit range expanded by 2*) to attacks by undead until the end of the ghoul's next turn.

Pound of flesh: The newly-risen ghoul's *scrabbling claws* attack deals +2 damage against vulnerable targets.

AC 17	
PD 15	**HP 9 (mook)**
MD 11	

Mook: Kill one newly-risen ghoul mook for every 9 damage you deal to the mob.

DWARF SKELETONS

"Creak . . . creak . . . creak."

1st level blocker [UNDEAD]
Initiative: +3
Vulnerability: holy

Bony punch +6 vs. AC—5 damage
 Natural even hit: The skeleton leaves bone fragments in the wound; the target takes 5 ongoing damage, and the dwarf skeleton takes 1d6 damage.

Persistent opponent: Enemies with a lower initiative count than the dwarf skeleton take a −5 penalty to disengage checks against it.

Resist weapon damage 16+: When a weapon attack targets this creature, the attacker must roll a natural 16+ on the attack roll or it only deals half damage.

Skilled intercept 11+: Once per round, an engaged dwarf skeleton can attempt to pop free and intercept an enemy moving past it. Roll a normal save; on an 11+, it succeeds.

AC 15	
PD 14	**HP 25**
MD 13	

JALEN

"You're gonna be ghoul meat, fool!"

1st level archer [HUMANOID]
Initiative: +4

Knife +5 vs. AC—4 damage
 Miss: 2 damage.

R: Crossbow +6 vs. AC—5 damage
 Natural even hit: The target is knocked off-balance, forcing a DC 15 skill check to keep its balance if in a precarious position (like on the bridge or edge of the pit).
 Natural 18+: The target takes 3 extra damage.

Wily: Jalen is quick and gains a +5 bonus to disengage checks.

AC 17	
PD 14	**HP 25**
MD 12	

GRAYSON, SEEKER MAGE

"You just made your last mistake!"

2nd level caster [HUMANOID]
Initiative: +5

Bone rod +6 vs. AC—6 damage

R: Forcebolt +7 vs. PD—7 force damage, and the target is knocked off-balance, forcing a DC 15 skill check to keep its balance if in a precarious position (like on the bridge or edge of the pit)

R: Graveblast +7 vs. PD (1d3 nearby enemies in a group)—4 negative energy damage
 Natural 16+: The target is vulnerable (save ends).

C: Ghostly hands +7 vs. MD (each enemy engaged with Grayson)—2 negative energy damage, and the target pops free from Grayson as the hands pull it away
 Limited use: 1/battle, as a quick action.

One step closer to death: When Grayson is staggered, his form becomes ghostly like a wraith until the end of the battle and he gains *resist damage 16+* to all damage except force damage.

AC 17	
PD 13	**HP 33**
MD 16	

 Loot: The ghouls and skeletons have nothing of value. Grayson has many small pouches and pockets full of spell components, as well as 25 gp and a pair of onyx rings: a skull ring worth 20gp, and one with silver-painted runes on the inside worth 10 gp. Neither is magical, but the runes on the second one signify danger and death. Grayson wears a tattered gray Arcanists of the Hidden Veil robe, but stored in one of the bedrooms is a rust-colored Lamplighter robe that's well-maintained with a brass chain with lantern at the end in one pocket (it's the Lamplighters' symbol).

Aftermath: In Grayson's robe pocket is a note that says, *"Ambrose, you did well with the cart. The attack achieved what we desired, though the fools who intervened reduced our expected output. Keep out of sight for now. When things calm down, come to the dreammaster's theater for the next delivery."* It's signed by Paulos (or if the PCs have already faced him, then one of the other Seeker agents), or if the group is ready for the next stage of their search, use Arlissa's name. If Grayson somehow escapes, the PCs find the note in one of the offices.

If Grayson is captured, he will only laugh maniacally at the PCs who try to interrogate him. This is because, as soon as he reveals any Seekers' secret, including their existence, a spell Garados placed on him will trigger. The spell is a curse that will cut off his breath and cause his tongue to turn to ash, filling his lungs and suffocating him before any countermeasures can be enacted. If he is tortured, he will trigger the curse on purpose.

The Lamplighter symbol on Grayson/Abrose might lead the PCs to the Lamplighter's Guild, since the symbol is common and known throughout the town. If the old brewery is the first lead the PCs follow, feel free to exclude this clue if you think it might send the PCs to the Lanternwerks too soon. As far as the guild members are concerned, no one knows anyone named Grayson. Abrose, however, is a member who's been on leave for a few weeks.

MISSED LEADS

If the PCs come to a dead end for some reason, it's a good time to have them roll icon relationship dice, or to use advantages from dice rolled at the start of the session. Successes indicate that new information comes to the PCs that will push them toward one of the unexplored adventure leads. The information should come with complications for any PC who rolls a 5, as normal. Feel free to reward multiple advantages with direct information about the

main leads that might bypass needing to talk to some NPCs, or by reducing enemies in a battle. Alternately, you could also have the PCs talk to street folk, government officials, Silver Shields, and the like, and roll skill checks as needed. Successes brings leads while failures mean that it takes more time or that enemies are more difficult but they learn what they need. Keep the action moving forward!

THE LAMPLIGHTER'S GUILD

At some point the PCs may want to visit the Lamplighter's Guild. Or perhaps they've finally found information connecting Arlissa Thent to the Seekers of the Lost and learn that she works at the Lanternwerks, the main office of the Lamplighter's Guild in the Saddle. In either case, they'll probably want to learn more about the guild.

Basic research into the Lamplighter's Guild will bring to light the guild's role in keeping Eldolan's streets and squares lit at night (in most districts). The PCs will also learn that the guild is run by the Kessmirs, an old and respected noble family of wizards, and specifically by the family's patriarch, Garados, who also runs a curiosity shop in the Grounds. The guild is based out of a place called the Lanternwerks in the Saddle.

If they seek out the guild's leader, their search will take them to the *Relic Hunter's Emporium*, the curiosity shop that Garados and Laredes run in the Grounds. The first time the PCs show up, Garados will be minding the store.

If the PCs' path instead takes them to the Lanternwerks, the guild wizards around the building will answer basic questions and generally be open and forthcoming (as much as any wizard is) if the PCs show them respect. But their answers shouldn't provide too much useful information beyond than the fact that Arlissa Thent is the head of the Lanternwerks, the guild's purpose is to

light the town at night, and that the building is much more active at night (especially around dusk) than in the day.

While Garados has installed some Seekers of the Lost within the Lamplighter's Guild, many in the guild are unaware of the darkness at its heart. They are only lesser wizards who have graduated from the Schools of Magic and found employment as Lamplighters (those who travel the town at night using their magic to light the lanterns) and lantern artificers (those who make the magic lanterns that hold a light spell all night). The Lamplighters wear their guild's rust-colored wizard robes, with lanterns stitched on the cuffs, and each has a Lamplighter chain around their neck to indicate their position.

If possible, have the PCs learn of the Kessmirs and Garados first before they gain any damming evidence against the Lamplighters—a meeting with Garados at the shop will provide dramatic foreshadowing to the later confrontation.

If the PCs are seeking to infiltrate the Lanternwerks, or if they have found a connection between Arlissa Thent and the attack and plan on attacking her and the guild, all of the guild members will oppose them unless the PCs manage to convince them of Arlissa's treachery (see **Facing Arlissa Thent**).

THE GROUNDS

The Grounds is the name given to the district that houses the buildings of the Schools of Magic. Students, faculty, and locals all name it so. Most of the district consists of the dormitories, classrooms, study halls, towers, laboratories, and other places for arcane study that fill the top of hill where each School resides. But there are a number of shops, a few taverns and inns, and other specialty locations catering to the wizard students built up around the edges of the district where it connects to the Saddle.

In addition to the many wizard students of all three schools always coming and going between the Grounds and the Saddle, those who have influence, or who have an official invite, can get past the mundane gate guards (and the magical protections they control) without any trouble. Anyone else will need to talk their way past "Shazurl's Door," the only gate into the Grounds. Of course, magical wards cover the walls and cliffs separating the district from the others, so bypassing the gate is difficult. Whether the PCs have to work for it to gain entrance, need to use an iconic advantage to do so, or have invites thanks to their iconic connections is up the GM.

Once past the gates, however, no one takes notice of strangers in the district, at least until they try to enter the school grounds directly—there are much stronger wards and guardians making sure only instructors and students can do so. (The Schools of Magic aren't outlined in this adventure, but feel free to flesh them out in whatever style you like and take the search for the Seekers through those varied and magical halls.)

Students wearing their school-colored robes are constantly moving about the Grounds, going from classrooms and labs to the taverns and shops and back again. The Grounds is the best-lit district in Eldolan, with a Lamplighter's lantern on almost every corner. The lanterns even use different colors of light to identify the boundaries of each School's area of influence (blue, speckled silver, golden yellow)

The *Relic Hunter's Emporium* sits near the wall that separates the Grounds from the Saddle, butted up against the edge of the lower cliffs overlooking Temples. Other shops with magical or semi-magical goods are spread out along the inner wall and cliffs around the emporium, including two different potion shops.

THE RELIC HUNTER'S EMPORIUM

Anyone who lives in the Grounds can give directions to the emporium. It has a wooden sign out front showing the Archmage's symbol (very common in the district) and an open chest with light pouring out above the name. It also says, "We buy, sell, and trade antiquities from the Ages."

The shop isn't large but it has a lot of shelves and nooks and crannies where "wonders" are waiting to be found. Most of the inventory will appeal to arcane spellcasters or those who like old lore. There's one entire bookshelf full of arcane tomes: histories (or stories) of the 13th Age as well as the last two previous ages,

ICON INVOLVEMENTS IN THE GROUNDS

A delegation of blue sorcerers, official representatives of Drakkenhall's Imperial governor (the Blue; one of the Three), have recently arrived in town to negotiate a trade agreement for magical components from the Iron Sea. But there have been altercations between the delegation's servants—lesser sorcerers who are functionaries and spies—and the Schools' students (Archmage) when the groups encounter each other in the Grounds. There hasn't been any outright dueling yet, but a few close calls. Some formal complaints have now also brought Imperial relations into it (Emperor).

While in the district, the PCs might witness a duel between wizards and sorcerers. They're either asked to join a side, or to be witnesses for one side or the other when the duel leads to a death and legal/political battles.

a few minor spellbooks, a scroll or two outlining useful rituals, and other similar manuscripts. There's also a small selection of non-magical wands, some well-used but comfortable hats, a display of wizard boxes (requires an *arcane mark* to open without destroying what's inside), and a wide array of oddities. Nothing in the store would suggest anything related to "dark magic" that the Archmage's people might frown upon (though there might be a few such items behind the counter).

Watch-sprites keep an eye on the merchandise, yelling out if someone looks like they're shoving something in a pocket, and the doorways are heavily inscribed with wards against theft (the proprietor's *arcane mark* must be placed on the item for it to leave the shop). The first time that the PCs go to the shop, Garados will be manning the counter.

MEETING GARADOS

Garados is a tall, thin human with an elongated face that ends in a medium-length black beard showing some gray. His skin is pale like most wizards who spend too much time indoors, and his robes are less rumpled than most of the wizards in the Grounds and made better: dark silver and rust-colored mistweave with gold stitching showing his family's crest (a lantern) on one sleeve and the mithril gear of the Mithril wizard school on the other, as well as the usual assortment of magical runes around the rest of it. He isn't one for hats and is balding in front but wears his stringy black hair long in back. His education and refinement show in his speech, which is slow and measured, though as he talks his right eye tends to twitch.

Unless he has spies following the PCs (due to a complication from a relationship check) or the characters have made open accusations against the guild at the Lanternwerks, Garados will assume they have come to the shop to buy and will introduce himself and give them the usual spiel. As soon as they start asking questions about the guild, or mention the zombie attack, he will become guarded, though he is quite skilled at deceiving people (he's been doing it since he was young) and any skill checks to determine if he's lying or holding something back, or to gage his reactions, have a DC of 25. (Try not to play Garados as "hiding something" upon a first meeting; he should seem like just another strange old wizard.)

If the PCs mention that they've found links between the Lamplighter's Guild and the recent attack in Hawker's Square, Garados will ask what sort of information they have. If the link is weak, he will dismiss it, saying that there have been a few guild members who didn't live up to its standards, and so were ousted, blaming malcontents for the trouble, or even racking it up to stolen robes, a common occurrence. If they have a letter or confession, he will mutter about how that's bad news indeed, talk about how it will be bad for business, and ask how he can help bring those who are responsible to justice, offering his full support. He'll say that he has a meeting with the Mage Council shortly about another matter but will offer the services of one of the guild officers, Arlissa Thent, at the Lanternwerks office to help them sort things out.

It's all lies of course. Once he gets the PCs out the door, he'll put plans in motion to have the Seekers get rid of them, possibly with Arlissa sending them into an ambush if they seek her "help." The key with this first meeting is to introduce Garados (as the future villain) and to have him deflect the PCs' suspicions away from him and the Guild. If for some reason the PCs attack Garados, he will attempt to flee rather than attack, and will head toward the school grounds, where a group of eight Mithril students will come to his aid (use Lamplighter Wizard stats) as he tries to escape by entering the school gates. His stats are at the end of the adventure, if needed, and he's more than a match for the PCs.

SEEKER AMBUSH

If the PCs shake the hornets' nest, so to speak, Garados or Arlissa will arrange for the Seekers to put an end to the heroes in the near future. Sometime over the next few hours or nights (don't stage it immediately after the meeting with Garados), the Seekers will ambush the PCs as they travel about town, preferably in one of the poorer, less guarded districts (it definitely won't happen in the Grounds or the Governs).

Whether it's in a small square, along the road, or on the piers, a Seeker wizard named Samuel and an assassin he hired, Nightshade, will try to put an end to the heroes. The battle will take some free-form planning on the GM's part to determine when and where the best time to hit the group will be, but it should occur once the sun goes down someplace where there aren't a lot of people who could witness the attack.

Read to the players: *As you make your way past dark buildings filled with the candlelight of townsfolk settling in for the night, the wizard-lantern lights easily guide your way through the streets. That is until they suddenly start to go out, one-after-another, in both directions away from you. As your eyes adjust to the ambient light, you see a robed figure wearing a skeletal-faced mask striding toward you. It's a man, a human, holding a handful of white sticks in each hand. In a low voice he says, "We have grown tired of your incursions. And so, useless as you are, we shall make use of you anyway. Well, your dead bodies at least!" as he flings the sticks—bones—upon the ground with a rattle and hisses out a word of power. The bones become skeletal warriors.*

Tactics: The bones have been ritually prepared, and as the wizard, **Samuel**, throws them to the ground, the magic makes them grow into **four skeleton warriors** holding ancient swords. They form a semi-circle in front of the wizard to intercept anyone that tries to reach him. On their first turn, three will engage the PCs while one remains back to intercept any enemy attempting to reach the wizard. But Samuel also has an ace up his sleeve; hidden on a nearby rooftop is **Nightshade**, a female drow assassin whose preferred attack is an arrow through the eye. She begins the battle away from the edge of a roof and will use move actions to move into firing position or out of sight each turn (so she's only visible to those on ground level every other round).

The ambush site can have whatever features you think best for the PCs, but there shouldn't be a lot of cover from Nightshade's attacks from above. Climbing to the roof of a nearby building requires a DC 15 Strength or Dexterity check, though Nightshade will try to shoot anyone doing so. If things don't go well, Samuel will use his *fog cloud* spell to beat a hasty retreat when he is under 10 hp, leaving the skeletons to finish the job. Any PC attempting to detect which way Samuel flees must succeed on a DC 15 Wisdom check. If no enemies have engaged Samuel by his next turn, he will escape thanks to the receding fog. **Roll initiative!**

If there are only 4 PCs, remove one skeleton warrior. If there are 6 PCs, add one skeleton warrior. There is no map for this battle since the GM could place it anywhere.

SKELETON WARRIOR

They move in unison, silently pointing their blades at you.

2nd *level troop* [UNDEAD]
Initiative: +8
Vulnerability: holy

Sword +8 vs. AC—6 damage

Resist weapons 16+: When a weapon attack targets this creature, the attacker must roll a natural 16+ on the attack roll or it only deals half damage.

AC	16	
PD	14	**HP 26**
MD	11	

NIGHTSHADE, ARCHER ASSASSIN

"....................."

2nd *level archer* [HUMANOID]
Initiative: +8

Hidden stiletto +7 vs. AC—5 damage

R: Shortbow +8 vs. AC—7 damage
  Natural 16+: The target takes +1d6 damage.
  Cruel critical: The crit range of Nightshade's ranged attacks expands by an amount equal to the escalation die.

Not paid enough for this: Once Nightshade is staggered, she will flee the battle (across the rooftops).

Mistress of the rooftops: While Nightshade is on higher ground than an enemy attacking her, she gains a +2 bonus to all defenses.

AC	17 (19)	
PD	15 (17)	**HP 36**
MD	12 (14)	

Loot: The skeletons revert to a few old bones when killed and have nothing of value. Nightshade never takes more than a few silvers with her on a job, but her stiletto has a cat's eye gem in the pommel and is worth 25 gp. Samuel has 10 gp in a pouch, various spell components, and a 20 gp silver medallion showing a one-eyed skull, which he wears around his neck under his clothes. He also bears the Lich King's symbol inked upon his chest over his heart—the Archmage's people will pay a standing 30 gp bounty for any Lich King follower bearing the symbol upon their flesh, dead or alive, if divination rituals cast upon the body prove the connection.

SAMUEL, SEEKER WIZARD

"Your dead flesh shall prove useful."

2nd *level caster* [HUMANOID]
Initiative: +4

Sharpened bone knife +5 vs. AC—5 damage

R: Force bolt +7 vs. PD—6 force damage
  Natural odd hit: Samuel can make a follow-up *magic missile* attack against one different target this turn as a quick action. He doesn't need to make an attack roll and the target takes 2d4 force damage.

R: Ray of exhaustion +7 vs. PD (1d2 enemies in a group) —4 negative energy damage, and the target loses its next move action
  Natural 16+: If the target has any temporary hit points, they are dispelled. In addition, until the end of the target's next turn, it only heals 50% of the hit points it would normally gain from using a recovery.
  Limited use: 2/ battle.

Fog cloud: Once per battle as a quick action, Samuel can fill the area with heavy fog that lasts until the end of his next turn. All checks to see or hear those in the cloud take a –5 penalty unless the creature is next to that person, and attacks against nearby or far away creatures (that can be seen) take a –4 penalty. In addition, disengage checks gain a +5 bonus.

Arcane shield: Once per battle as a free action, when a ranged attack hits Samuel, he only takes half damage from the attack.

AC	16	
PD	13	**HP 33**
MD	16	

Aftermath: If Samuel is captured, he won't talk. Even if threatened with death, he won't say anything (seeing death as a way to serve the Lich King). Torture might get some information out of him, but it will take some time. Nightshade is less fervent and more of a hired hand than a true Seeker, though she knows a few things about the group. She'll be willing to deal her information for her freedom if the PCs can convince her they'll stick to the bargain (through roleplaying or with a successful DC 15 skill check).

Nightshade knows that some Seekers mainly work out of the Lanternwerks in the Saddle, but they take orders from some wizard in the Grounds (she **doesn't** know Garados' name, but does know that Arlissa Thent ordered Samuel to ambush the group if you're ready to move to the next stage of the story). She also knows that not all the Lamplighters are Seekers.

THE LANTERNWERKS

The Lanternwerks is a two-story, rectangular brick building with an attached three-story round tower on one end in the Saddle district. The upper floors are offices and meeting chambers, and it also has a sub-level below the street surface where the artificers work in a large, sub-divided shop that fills most of the floor. There are two obvious entrances: the main door (a large, strong-looking iron door), and the side entrance in the tower (iron-reinforced wood; always barred). There's also a trapdoor through the tower roof that isn't obvious. At each of the building's corners, a large iron lantern in the style of those that dot the town glows with wizard light at night. In addition, a much larger lantern with an eye-pleasing orange glow extends from the top of the tower, identifying the Lanternwerks to all.

The main door is open to visitors during daylight hours. An older guild wizard keeps an eye out for people (or has magical sprites inform him of arrivals). People go there to report lanterns whose magic is failing, or to purchase custom lanterns for homes or businesses (nobles, merchants, clergy).

The building shows little activity during the day, especially in the morning since many of the wizards work from dusk to midnight lighting lanterns. Wizards arrive for their shifts during the late afternoon, then head out into the town. The artificers work on new lamps and other lighting magic during the day and early evening in the bowels of the building. So depending on the time of day or night, the place can be full of wizards or nearly empty.

ENTERING THE LANTERNWERKS

Once the PCs learn about Arlissa Thent and her connection to those who orchestrated the attack, the Seekers of the Lost, reaching her might be a little tricky for them. Arlissa is installed at the Lanternwerks as a ranking member of the Lamplighter's Guild, a well-respected organization in town. She stays at the Lanternwerks most of the time, serving as an administrator who assigns wizards to their lamplighting duties each week (allowing her to place Seeker members where and when she needs them). She won't leave the building for at least a week after the attacks since Garados told her to stay there to avoid attention. If some action the PCs take does force her to report to Garados, she will use a secret exit from the basement of the Lanternwerks to leave unnoticed.

Since she's staying inside the Lanternwerks, the PCs will need to go there to confront her and learn more about the Seekers. If they do, there's three primary ways to go about it— the direct approach fighting their way in, or two other options: sneaking in or talking their way in. See the map on page 55 for a layout of the building's three levels.

USING THE AUTHORITIES

There is another way for the PCs to try to get to Arlissa: they could try to involve the authorities, namely the Silver Shields or the Mage Council. It won't be subtle and might expose the icon they're working for to unwanted publicity, but it is an option. Unless they have damning evidence of Arlissa's involvement in the attack, however, that ploy is unlikely to work. Arlissa and guild are well-connected in the town, and she will call in favors and political allies. Plus the Silver Shields have their hands full. The authorities, such as they are, will tell the PCs to drop it after a day or two of discussions because their involvement is causing waves. Having a letter from one of the Seeker agents that names Arlissa won't count as strong enough evidence in the eyes of the Mage Council, either, since anyone's name can be written down on a piece of parchment. In other words, the odds are stacked against the heroes.

Of course, once the PCs have made accusations and/or shown themselves to be a nuisance, Arlissa will order the Seeker ambush against them lead by Samuel (if she or Garados hasn't already done so).

Fighting Their Way In

If the PCs try to bash their way into the building, they might have to deal with a lot of angry wizards. Since not all guild members are part of the Seekers, some innocent wizards might end up getting hurt or killed, and it could turn into a political nightmare for the icon the PCs are working for. This doesn't mean the heroes can't take this option, but there will be consequences. At the least, it would be a good idea for PCs to assault the place when it's least active, just after dusk when most of the guild members are on the streets. If they try the direct approach when the place is full, add a battle of 3d4 lamplighter wizard mooks (see page 54) to the other battles at the Lanternwerks. These wizards will defend the building from the roof, street, and/or main entrances as the PCs try to force their way inside. If you like, include Keloris, the Lamplighter head wizard (who's not a Seeker), in the battle. You can find her information in the NPC Stats at the back of the adventure.

Once the PCs get inside, Arlissa and her Seeker friends will be waiting for them. Go to **Searching for Arlissa** for more information on those battles.

Sneaking In

There are four entrances to the building: the main door, the tower door, the trapdoor on the tower roof, and a secret door from one of the basement storage rooms into a tunnel that exits into a nearby alley in the Saddle. Only the Seekers in the guild know about the secret exit, though it could be that shadowy types in the Saddle also know about it and inquiring PCs who are willing to pay 50 gp (and who succeed at a DC 20 skill check or use an advantage from an icon roll) can learn about it.

The main door is open during the day, but a wizard watches over the place and controls the locks on a second interior door. During the evening hours it's closed and locked (DC 20 to bypass), and has a guardian watch-sprite (small blue-skinned goblin) that will cry out in alarm if anyone tries to jimmy the lock and fails (or if anyone bashes it in). The wizards use a magic catchphrase to gain entrance during off-hours, however, and stealthy PCs listening in (a DC 15 check) can overhear it without being seen. The phrase is: *Limwit's flame*. The door opens and the watch-sprite remains asleep for anyone using the phrase.

The tower door is barred and requires a DC 20 check to jimmy open or bust down. A failure at picking the lock or busting it open will make noise and draw the attention as the heroes gain entrance. The trapdoor on the tower roof is unlocked, but climbing the outside of the tower requires a successful DC 15 skill check; once the first PC is up, they can help the others without needing rolls if someone has a rope. Failure doesn't result in falling (though a fumble might), but the PCs make a lot of noise and a wizard mook from the inside will come out to investigate, perhaps requiring DC 15 skill checks for stealth from each character to avoid notice.

If the PCs gain access to the Lanternwerks without alerting anyone, go to **Searching For Arlissa** for more information on what they face inside the building. If they do alert those inside, they'll first have to deal with 2d4 Lamplighter wizard mooks who arrive at the door the PCs are entering in addition to any other battles.

Talking Their Way In

The main outer door stays open until about an hour after dusk. Inside is a small waiting room with some benches and a pull-rope. Pulling the rope summons one of the older guild wizards. Also, if anyone tries to open the interior door from the waiting room into the rest of the Lanternwerks, a magical pixie-like female sprite will appear and yell very loudly, "Show some patience and sit down! Master, master, there are visitors!" An old gnome Lamplighter named Cornelius will enter through the inner door and ask the PCs their business.

This is the PCs' opportunity to creatively figure out a way to get a meeting with Arlissa, or at least to get inside the main building. As long as the heroes aren't making overtures of wanting to hurt Arlissa or anyone in the guild, Cornelius won't be suspicious and it will be easier to gain access, requiring DC 15 skill checks. If they are threatening Cornelius or another guild member, or making accusations, he gets crotchety and any checks are now DC 20. It will take three successful checks, each from a different PC making a case, to gain entry. With each failure, Cornelius will become slightly more suspicious of the PCs (make it obvious to the players). Cornelius does have a weakness for good pranks, however, and especially magical pranks. If someone gets him talking about them, PCs making checks to talk him into letting them in gain a +4 bonus to the roll.

For each skill check failure, the battle against Arlissa will be more difficult: add one Seeker imposter to the battle (to a maximum of 3, see **Facing Arlissa Thent**). Cornelius will eventually relent, saying that Arlissa should sort it out, and he will summon a guide-sprite that looks like a small golden-green owl to lead the PCs to Arlissa's office; he has to keep manning the door and doesn't suspect them of mischief.

Alternately, PCs with relationship dice with the Archmage could use previously rolled advantages or make a new roll rather than use skill checks: one advantage (a 5 or 6) will gain the group entry into the building with Cornelius directing one of the guild wizards inside to take them to Arlissa, and two or more advantages means that Cornelius will summon the guide-sprite owl to lead them to Arlissa. Of course, one obvious complication would be for Cornelius to also use a *message* spell to tell Arlissa that the PCs are coming, letting her prepare by adding two imposters to the battle.

MEETING ARLISSA BEFORE THE PCs KNOW SHE'S A SEEKER

There's a chance that the PCs go to the Lanternwerks early in their investigation after they find a connection between the attack and the guild, or when Garados sends them there to help find "the perpetrators." If that happens, let them meet with Arlissa without any checks to learn about the guild while she learns about their investigation. The PCs should have no inkling that she's involved in any way, and she'll offer to help in any way she can. It will be good foreshadowing to their later confrontation. If Garados sent the PCs to her, she'll set up the Seeker ambush and point them toward a false clue (like the cultists in the Docks).

SEARCHING FOR ARLISSA

If the PCs managed to convince Cornelius to allow them to talk to Arlissa, he will send them to her office following either an owl-sprite or one of the guild wizards. In this case, the PCs are taken to her office directly and won't have the following encounter (go to **Facing Arlissa Thent**). If the PCs have instead snuck or fought their way into the Lanternwerks, they will need to track Arlissa

down to confront her. Arlissa's office is on the second floor, opposite the tower. Before the PCs encounter Arlissa, however, they may have to deal with a mixed group of Lamplighter wizards and Seeker imposters still in the building who will attack first and ask questions later (in addition to any Lamplighter wizards they might have had to face getting inside). Preferably the PCs encounter them on the ground floor or near the tower on the second level.

Tactics: At some point as they roam the building, the PCs will have to get past this group of **six Lamplighter wizards** and **two Seeker imposters**. If the PCs aren't using stealth or subterfuge, this group will definitely see them (or run into them) and order them to drop their weapons and surrender. Otherwise a stealthy/tricky group might be able to bypass this battle. In that case, have each PC roll a DC 15 check. If at least half of them succeed, they can bypass this battle. Reward cleverness with bonuses to the check. If there is a battle, choose a location that gives the PCs some options for fun movement rather than a narrow corridor (perhaps it could occur within a handful of rooms and a main corridor).

If it comes to a fight, a battle against this group shouldn't be that tough. If any player questions whether they should be killing the wizards, remind them that the PCs can choose to deliver non-lethal blows when a foe drops, assuming that would make sense for the attack used. The imposters' negative energy attacks and/or skeletal visages might cause concern among the Lamplighter wizards who survive the battle and sway them to the PCs' story after the battle.

If there are only 4 PCs, remove two Lamplighter wizards. If there are 6 PCs, add another Seeker imposter. Once the imposters have dropped and can no longer encourage their comrades, the wizards might consider surrender.

LAMPLIGHTER WIZARD

"You shouldn't be here!"

2ⁿᵈ level mook [HUMANOID]
Initiative: +5

Guild knife +6 vs. AC—3 damage

R: Elemental ray +7 vs. PD—5 damage of the following type: acid, cold, fire, or lightning (GM choice)
Natural even hit: The target takes 2 ongoing damage of the same type.

Group ability: For every two Lamplighter wizard mooks in the battle (round up), one of them can use *shocking discharge* as a quick action (once per round) during the battle.

Shocking discharge (group): Each enemy engaged with the wizard takes 2 lightning damage and pops free from the wizard.

AC	**17**	
PD	**11**	**HP 8 (mook)**
MD	**15**	

Mook: Kill one Lamplighter wizard mook for every 8 damage you deal to the mob.

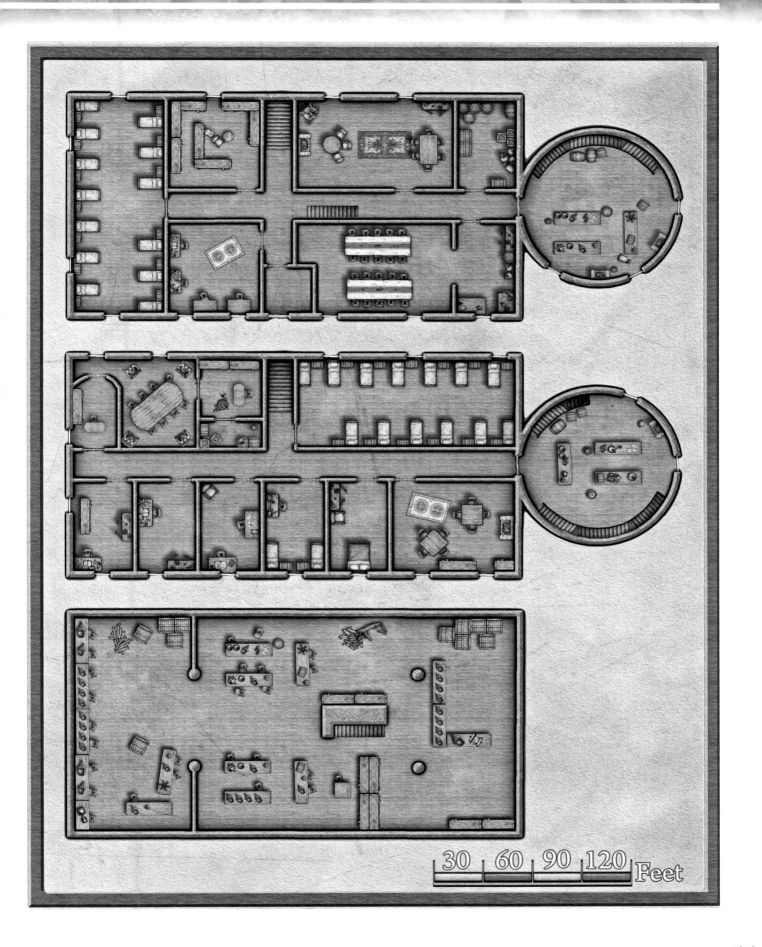

30 60 90 120 Feet

SEEKER IMPOSTER

"Kill the thieves!"

2ⁿᵈ level caster [HUMANOID]
Initiative: +5

Staff +7 vs. AC—5 damage

R: Draining ray +8 vs. PD—5 negative energy damage, and the
target is hampered until the end of its next turn
Natural even hit: The target is also vulnerable until the end of
its next turn.

Lich King's tricks: Once per battle as a free action, when a weapon
attack hits the imposter, it gains *resist weapon damage 16+*
(attacker using a weapon must roll natural 16+ on the attack
roll or the attack only deals half damage) against that attack as
it channels the undead power of skeletons. The imposter's face
and hands will take on skeletal features for the rest of the battle
when it does this.

AC	**18**	
PD	**12**	**HP 30**
MD	**16**	

Loot: Each wizard carries 1d4 gp, plus an assortment of spell
components, but little else of real value. The imposters each have
10 gp and bear a small Lich King tattoo somewhere on their body.

Aftermath: Any surviving Lamplighter's Guild members
could be persuaded to direct the PCs to Arlissa's office with a
successful DC 15 skill check. Give them a +5 bonus if the PC
mentions the imposters' unnatural spells/appearance. Failure
means the wizards will condemn the PCs as intruders and thieves
there to steal the guild's secrets and they won't help. The PCs
may have to spend a few minutes searching, but they will still
eventually find Arlissa's office, though you could add an extra
imposter to the fight in that case.

FACING ARLISSA THENT

If the PCs successfully talked their way into the Lanternwerks,
they will be lead directly to Arlissa's offices. Otherwise, they will
have to search the building or get her location from a captured
guild member to find her. The upper floors will be conveniently
empty of guild wizards, though if the PCs bypassed the wizards
and imposters, sounds of battle might bring the group to the fray
after four rounds if you want to really challenge the PCs.

Arlissa is in her suite of offices. The outer door from the hall
connects to her scribe's office, a small 20 by 20 foot room with a
simple wooden desk holding inks and quills and two floor-to-
ceiling bookshelves of ledgers and business documents. Her scribe
is currently away on business. An open archway connects to a 40
by 30 foot meeting room with a heavy, wooden oval table and eight
chairs. Four gargoyle statues reside in each corner of the room in
different poses. At the far end, a closed door separates the meeting
room from Arlissa's office. It's a spacious 30 by 20 foot room adorned
with three bookshelves along one wall, a few display cases showing
preserved monster parts, and a heavy black oak writing desk
holding quills and inks, with a side cabinet for storing documents.

Depending on the method in which the PCs entered the
Lanternwerks, Arlissa may be waiting for the PCs or not, and she
may have additional support.

- If the PCs talked their way in without failing any checks and
are following a messenger owl, she won't have any Seeker
imposters with her.
- If the PCs talked their way in without failing any checks and
are following a guild wizard or were warned by Cornelius that
she has visitors, she will have one Seeker imposter with her
(the guide if there is one, or another waiting with her).
- If the PCs talked their way in but failed some checks, there
will be one Seeker imposter for each failure (max 3), in
addition to any others.
- If the PCs snuck in and managed to bypass the wizards and
imposters battle, she won't have any Seeker imposters with her
- If the PCs snuck in and ended up battling the wizards and
imposters, she will have two Seeker imposters with her, and
potentially a third if they try to make the wizards reveal where
Arlissa is at but fail and take extra time.
- If the PCs fought their way in, she will have two Seeker
imposters with her.
- No matter which method the PCs use, she should not have
more than four Seeker imposter allies with her. If there are
four, it'll be a very difficult fight. Consider having one with her
and bringing in each additional imposter during a new round.

If Arlissa has been informed of the PCs approach via a
messenger sprite, if they fought their way in, or if they didn't
bypass the battle while searching for her, she will be waiting
in the meeting room with her allies. Otherwise, she'll be at her
office desk busy writing a report. If the PCs were escorted to the
office by a guild member, that member will be a Seeker imposter
who will stay and attack from behind. Adjust the following text
as necessary if the PCs meet Arlissa in her office, if she has more
allies, or if they are meeting her on friendly terms before knowing
of her involvement, in which case she'll be alone.

Read to the players: *Beyond the archway of the small
office is a rectangular room with a large, thick oval table in
the center. Chairs are pushed in around it and four statues of
gargoyles adorn each corner of the chamber. There's also an
open door at the far end of the room that leads to an office.
Standing in front of the door by the table is a tall human
woman with pale skin and rich black hair. She has a narrow
face and small chin, with sparkling blue eyes, and a look of
annoyance on her face. In a high-pitched, shrill voice she says,
"Who are you? What do you want?"*

Unless the PCs immediately attack, Arlissa will play it cool.
She'll ask what the heroes want with her. She will do her best to
portray herself as innocent, or a victim of slander based on what
the PCs accuse her of. If they have a letter from one of the Seekers
with her name on it and/or seem intent on fighting or "getting
some answers," Arlissa will sigh, then say: *"Your persistence in
this is annoying. It's high time you were introduced to our lord . . .
permanently."* **Roll initiative!**

Tactics: In addition to any **Seeker imposter** allies she has with her, **Arlissa Thent** has a few tricks she can play. There are **two lesser gargoyles** among the statues that she can command with a quick action, which she will do during her first turn (they act immediately after Arlissa in initiative order). She will save *wizard's jaunt* to get away from melee-focused PCs who are trying to lock her down (or use it once to escape from her office into the meeting room on her first turn to get some space). Arlissa's primary attack, *screaming ghost skulls*, creates a spray of skull-shaped force magic infused with spiritual energy from those she's killed. If losing badly, Arlissa will try to flee or negotiate her way out if she can. If she dies, the gargoyles will stop fighting and any imposters will start thinking about fleeing unless the PCs look beatable.

The table is tall and thick, and it offers some cover to those hiding under/behind it, if you wish (a +2 bonus to all defenses). Using it for attack moves, or to try to get around defenders without them intercepting requires a successful DC 15 skill check (probably Str or Dex), though just moving up onto it doesn't. Also feel free to let the action spill out into the hallways and other rooms of the building to allow PCs to use the terrain, although it could draw more enemies if you feel like making things really tough on the PCs.

If there are only 4 PCs, remove one lesser gargoyle. If there are 6 PCs, add one lesser gargoyle. This battle can range from hard (Arlissa and 2 lesser gargoyles) to extremely challenging (up to 4 extra Seeker imposters).

ARLISSA THENT

"Your interference is going to cause problems for me."

Double-strength 3rd level caster [HUMANOID]
Initiative: +8

Staff +7 vs. AC—15 damage

R: Screaming ghost skulls +8 vs. PD (1d3 nearby enemies in a group)—6 force damage, and 5 ongoing negative energy damage
Natural 16+: The target also takes 5 ongoing psychic damage as it hears the screams of the dying.
Miss: 3 ongoing negative energy damage.

Dedicated to the Lich King: When Arlissa drops to 0 hp, she doesn't die until the end of her next turn (but make it clear she took a mortal blow). Dark shadows/spirits swirl about her keeping her on her feet and with her final death rattle, she can use *screaming ghost skulls* against 1d6 nearby enemies during her next turn before she expires (no matter how much damage she takes).

Forced servitude of the damned: Two times per battle as a free action (but only once per round), when a non-critical attack would hit Arlissa, she can call upon one of the spirits of those she's killed and forced to serve her. The spirit interposes itself between Arlissa and the attacker, and the attacker must reroll the attack. Each time she does this, reduce all *screaming ghost skulls* damage by 1 (including the ongoing, trigger, and miss damage).

Wizard jaunt: Twice per battle as a move action, Arlissa can teleport anywhere nearby that she can see.

AC	17	
PD	13	**HP 75**
MD	18	

LESSER GARGOYLE

The gargoyle stands and unfurls itself, cocking its head in your direction.

3rd level blocker [CONSTRUCT]
Initiative: Immediately after Arlissa

Piercing claws +7 vs. AC (2 attacks)—4 damage, and the target takes a −5 penalty to disengage checks against the gargoyle until the end of its next turn
Natural 16+: The gargoyle can make a *fangs* attack against the target as a free action.
[Special trigger] **Fangs +8 vs. AC**—5 damage

Stone hide: When an attacker hits the gargoyle with a natural odd melee attack roll, the attack only deals half damage.

AC	20	
PD	18	**HP 36**
MD	12	

SEEKER IMPOSTER

"Long live the one-eyed lord!"

2ⁿᵈ level caster [HUMANOID]
Initiative: +5

Staff +7 vs. AC—5 damage

R: Draining ray +8 vs. PD—5 negative energy damage, and the target is hampered until the end of its next turn
Natural even hit: The target is also vulnerable until the end of its next turn.

Lich King's tricks: Once per battle as a free action, when a weapon attack hits the imposter, it gains *resist weapon damage 16+* (attacker must roll natural 16+ on the attack roll or the attack only deals half damage) against that attack as it channels the undead power of skeletons. The imposter's face and hands will take on a skeletal outlook when it does this.

AC	18	
PD	12	**HP 31**
MD	16	

Loot: The gargoyles have no obvious valuables, although each of their eyes is a 50 gp onyx gem (4 or 6 total) if someone thinks to dig them out. If there are imposters, each carries 1d4 gp. Arlissa has some valuables, although any Lamplighter's Guild wizards present might not be happy with people looting her body (if they witness it) until all the facts about her involvement in the attack come out; once they learn the truth, they'll probably be more than willing to give away her things to help with the damage control of the guild being tied to the Lich King. There are 20 gp in a pouch in her desk, as well as a gold quill holder worth another 25 gp. She also has a few nice pieces of jewelry she wears, including a pair of jade thumb rings worth 40 gp each, a gold hair band of a bat worth 20 gp, and a simple, thin gold bracelet worth 60 gp. In a pouch at her side she carries a **Potion of Fire Resistance**, and she wears a pair of black leather **Gloves of Mind Rot**.

Arlissa bears the Lich King's symbol over her heart, and the Archmage's people will pay a bounty of 30 gp for her, dead or alive, when divinations prove she's tied to the Lich King.

Aftermath: If Arlissa is somehow captured alive, she's been enspelled against revealing anything about the Seekers of the Lost with a spell that causes her lungs to fill with gravedirt if she tries to reveal any of their secrets or mentions the spell upon her. A search through her personal belongings and her desk will reveal a number of items that, when seen as a group, make it obvious that she served the Lich King and not the Archmage (in addition to the tattoo over her heart). If the PCs fought their way into the Lanternwerks, this evidence could be important if more guild wizards show up looking for a fight.

One piece of evidence about the attacks is more damning than the rest, however, and it will also reveal to the PCs that Arlissa is not the Seekers' leader. There is a letter in the desk drawer to her from Garados. It says: *"Arlissa, all is prepared for the attack in the square. Abrose has the cart ready and will target the mark. Sigmund and Paulos will take our castoffs to the sewer-*

entry chamber and stage them the night before. If my projections are correct, more than 30 dead will be sent to the Vaults. Landon should be able to send at least five to my lab from there immediately without anyone missing them. The One-eyed Lord shall be pleased with the carnage and it shall serve my purposes also. Please coordinate the final details for me and send one of our people to the emporium for the wording key to trigger the zombies."

Hopefully the PCs have already met Garados, so that they will know of the emporium. If they haven't met Garados but did research the Lamplighter's Guild, they will be aware that the patriarch of the Kessmir family who runs the guild is named Garados and that he owns a shop called the *Relic Hunter's Emporium*. They can also learn that information from any surviving Lamplighter wizards. No matter how they learn of it, their next step will most likely be to go to the *Relic Hunter's Emporium* in the Grounds to confront Garados.

This would be a good time for the characters to get a full heal-up, before entering the Seeker's lair. If the action has fallen so that the PCs took a full heal-up right before this battle, then they'll have a tougher time of it against Garados.

BACK TO THE EMPORIUM

Once the PCs have defeated Arlissa Thent, the next time they go to the *Relic Hunter's Emporium* (presumably to confront Garados about the attacks), they will meet his business partner, Laredes the Sage.

Laredes is tall and thin with dirty blond hair and a goatee. He has pale skin, though it has a touch of color, and his robes are well-pressed and made from mithril-gray silk. His family's crest, a falcon, shows from his right breast in gold thread and he bears the mithril gear of the Mithril School upon one sleeve. He wears a cotton karakul hat and speaks with a refined voice in quick bursts. Laredes has been "friends" with Garados since their days at the School of Magic, but he is not a Seeker. Garados sees value in him for his legitimacy with the Archmage.

How the encounter with Laredes goes depends on what the PCs do once they get to the shop. Accusations about Garados being a Seeker and his orchestration of the attack in the square will be met with confusion by Laredes, and perhaps anger. Remember, he's never met the PCs before, and if any of them are aggressive toward him he will become defensive. It's best to play Laredes as wanting to figure out what the PCs are talking about, and he will be patient if provided both a logical story and a semblance of proof (like the note at Arlissa's). If the players are less confident in their verbal skills, you could leave it up to their characters and the dice, though roleplaying the situation should be more fun. Make it DC 25 to start with to convince Laredes, but add +5 if they show him Arlissa's note, and another +5 if they recap the events that lead them to Garados.

Alternately, you could allow PCs who have a positive or conflicted relationship with the Archmage to roll their relationship dice or use previous advantages. One or more such advantages will put some weight upon the PCs' story and get

Laredes' attention, making him compliant. He is, in the end, a servant of the Archmage and against dark magic. And though he sees Garados as a business partner, he knows the wizard would be a powerful servant for the Lich King if there's truth to what the heroes claim, and his duty would be to stop Garados.

Failed checks or relationship dice shouldn't stop the action, but they will limit Laredes' involvement. If the PCs convince him of Garados' part in the attack, he will help them fully and tell them about the secret passage Garados has in the shop that he doesn't think Laredes knows about. Otherwise, he will plan on confronting Garados on his own and in his own way, but he will suggest to the PCs that while he thinks they are mistaken about Garados' involvement, whoever wrote the note must have

a lab connected to the Dead Vaults. What other way could that Landon person move five bodies without raising questions? It's the only obvious answer.

There is a secret tunnel from the Dead Vaults to Garados' laboratory, and given time (a day or two of searching), the PCs will find it if they can convince Odessa to allow them to look, but that will give Garados time to prepare (add two human zombies to the battle with Garados). The best option for the PCs is learning about Garados' secret tunnel out of the shop from Laredes.

In the worst case scenario, the PCs annoy Laredes to the point that he won't help them. At that point, the PCs will have to find some other way to track down Garados (who will be keeping a low profile) and the adventure becomes totally free-form.

THE SEEKERS OF THE LOST

Garados created the Seekers of the Lost after his initial forays into learning dark magic that only the Lich King could teach him. With the help of his familiar, Kos, a servant the Lich King sent to Garados after he completed a special ritual of summoning, Garados learned many dark secrets and grew in power. Over the years, he found others who had similar interests and imparted some of his knowledge upon them for their obedience. Some were wizards, who he incorporated into his family's business, the Lamplighter's Guild. Others he has installed elsewhere in the town as independent agents of the Seekers working toward the group's ends.

In the time he had, Garados created a lair for the Seekers in which they could secretly meet. He discovered forgotten chambers among the ruins below the Grounds from the town's ancient days and had passages excavated from them to a few locations in Eldolan, including his curiosity shop in the Grounds, the Dead Vaults in the Temple district, the hidden passage connecting the Lanternwerks to an alley in the Saddle, and Griffin square, a small courtyard in the Commons that butts up against the cliff wall leading up to the Grounds (behind a griffin statue).

After meeting the heroes the first time, or after word of Arlissa Thent's defeat reaches him, Garados will realize that the PCs are getting close to discovering his involvement in the zombie attack at Hawker's Square, as well as the fact that he leads the Seekers. So he will work diligently to complete his latest project using a ritual that the One-eyed Lord's necromancers gave him in exchange for orchestrating the zombie attack—how to combine and animate the dead flesh of humanoids into a magical construct that will serve its master. The experiment is almost complete, and he is sequestered in his laboratory to finish the work. That's where he'll be when the PCs come for him.

WRONG TURNS

If the PCs fail to convince Laredes to help them, and also fail to discover any of the entrances to the Seekers' lair, rather than have the action suddenly end, either allow the PCs to use existing icon story-guide advantages or have the PCs roll new icon relationship dice for that purpose specifically.

If a player suggests using one or more of their story-guide advantages to gain the information, have that PC get the information about Garados' secret lair and how to access it from a fitting representative of that icon, such as directly from a sprite or other magical messenger or as a flashback dream that didn't make sense to the PC until that moment.

If the PCs roll new icon dice, give the information to the character who rolls the most successes, in a manner that fits their icon relationship.

If the PCs are still at a dead end because of failed rolls, consider having an agent of the Priestess provide the information during a divination, but in exchange for a quest-type favor on the group's part.

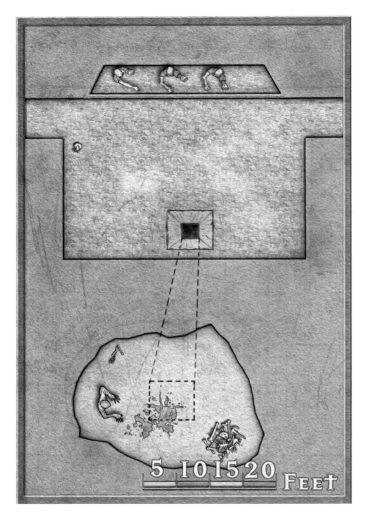

5 10 15 20 FEET

ENTERING THE SEEKERS' LAIR

If the PCs enter the Seekers' lair through the curiosity shop, the door is behind a bookshelf in a back room. Beyond, a short wooden stairway leads to a set of stone steps carved through the rock floor circling downward. After perhaps 200 steps, the stairway ends at a tunnel leading into darkness. The tunnel eventually enters into a medium-sized octagonal chamber. If the PCs come through another entrance, they will end up in the same chamber but coming from one of the other exits.

There are four other exits from the chamber, each a tunnel leading to the other parts of town. There are three exits on the left: one to the tunnel connecting the Lanternwerks to an alley in the Saddle; one to the Dead Vaults in Temples; and one to Griffin Square in the Commons. The last exit is on the right and leads to Garados' laboratory. (As a nexus point, there could be other tunnels here leading to more areas you've chosen to add, such as the Schools of Magic or the Docks.)

The tunnels to the other parts of the town hold no dangers and end at secret doors with peep holes to the other side. It will take a short amount of time to explore each tunnel to its end. The tunnel to the Seeker's lair and laboratory is more dangerous. The Seekers placed guardians in a chamber it bisects in case anyone managed to access their lair.

GHOUL PIT

As the PCs move down the tunnel toward the Seekers' lair they will detect the foul stench of carrion from ahead even before coming to the 30 by 20 foot rectangular chamber the smell is coming from. The chamber is constructed from mortared gray brick with a flagstone floor. There is one exit out the other end of the room, but at the center of the left wall, there's an 8 by 8 foot square shaft in the floor (see map at left). The stench fills the area, and the room holds nothing else of interest.

Tactics: While it's true that the carrion stench is partially coming from the shaft, which drops 15 feet down to a small chamber below the room, it's not the only source. This room holds **three human zombie guardians** standing along the wall to the right who are hidden by an illusion of a false wall. When anyone enters the chamber without uttering the correct phrase ("*I serve to discover the lost secrets.*"), the zombies will attack. But instead of simply slamming intruders into a bloody pulp, they've been instructed to grab their target and shuffle both themselves and their victim into the shaft. Unless the PCs are very careful or observant (DC 25 for those searching to note some telltale sign), the zombies should be able to surprise the heroes due to the magical concealment (using the standard surprise rules). As with the zombies in the square, these bodies have also been cut open and are missing organs.

Any creature (including the zombies) that falls into the shaft takes 2d6 damage. If a zombie hurls itself and an enemy into the pit, the zombie will begin to make *rotting fist* attacks against the target at that point. There is another problem, however, because Garados keeps a **ghoul** trapped in the pit, and it's hungry! It will lunge out of the shadows to feast. It will start attacking a zombie if that is the only meat that comes down into the pit, but it prefers fresher food if a PC comes down. The shaft is in the middle of the pit's ceiling with the bottom of the shaft 10 feet up, and attempts to climb the smooth, mold-covered walls to escape it are difficult (DC 25 Strength check) without help.

If there are only 4 PCs, remove one human zombie guardian. If there are 6 PCs, add one human zombie guardian.

HUMAN ZOMBIE GUARDIANS

"Mmmmmm"

2nd *level troop* [UNDEAD]
Initiative: +1
Vulnerability: holy

Grab and drag +8 vs. PD—The zombie grabs the target and drags/pushes it toward the pit
  Drag and drop: As part of the attack, the zombie will try to hurl itself and the target into the pit. The target can resist by making a DC 15 Strength or Dexterity check, but still remains grabbed if it succeeds. The zombie will continue making this attack or trying to drag a grabbed target into the pit (standard action that forces the check) until it succeeds, and then it will attack normally with *rotting fist.*
  Natural 16+: The zombie manages to hurl itself and the target into the pit without the target getting to make a skill check.

Rotting fist +7 vs. AC—6 damage
  Natural 16+: Both the zombie and its target take 1d6 damage!

Headshot: A critical hit against a zombie drops it to 0 hp.

AC	15	
PD	13	HP 52
MD	10	

GHOUL

Sniff. Sniff. Scrabble. Crunch!

3rd *level spoiler* [UNDEAD]
Initiative: +8
Vulnerability: holy

Claws and bite +8 vs. AC—8 damage
  Natural even hit: The target is vulnerable (*attacks vs. it have crit range expanded by 2*) to attacks by undead until the end of the ghoul's next turn.

Paralyzing bite: When the ghoul hits a vulnerable target with a natural even attack roll, the target is also stunned (save ends).

Pound of flesh: The ghoul's *claws and bite* attack deals +4 damage against vulnerable targets.

Infected bite: Any creature that is slain by a ghoul and not consumed will rise as a ghoul the next night.

AC	18	
PD	16	HP 36
MD	12	

Loot: The zombies have nothing of value. The ghoul only has a dwindling pile of gnawed-on bones in one corner from which it has sucked the marrow.

Aftermath: Getting out of the pit out of combat is easy using a rope or standing on someone's shoulders. The residual energy from the magical ritual that was used to create the illusionary wall will be obvious to an arcane spellcaster who succeeds on a DC 15 check to look for it once they realize the zombies were magically hidden. (It's also a DC 15 check to notice it ahead of time for a spellcaster PC who looks for magic in the room before entering; those who succeed will notice that an illusion is in place, but not see the zombies unless their check is 20 or higher.)

USING ICON ADVANTAGES

This fight with the ghoul, the battle with Garados and the flesh golem that follows, and even the fight against Arlissa to a lesser extent could each be very deadly if things go badly for the heroes. These are great times for the PCs to pull out those icon advantages they have to swing things in their favor.

For example, in this battle, if one PC is trapped in the pit and paralyzed by the ghoul, it could be a short career for that PC. Somebody with advantageous relationship dice with the Priestess or Lich King, or even one of the other icons with a good story, should be able to find a way to help the heroes overcome the situation. It may come at a price, but that only makes the save more interesting.

ENTERING GARADOS' LABORATORY

Beyond the ghoul pit chamber, the tunnel continues for another hundred feet before it ends at a large, ironbound wooden door that's closed. Inscribed upon the door is the Seeker's symbol, a skull with one eye searching. Beyond lies Garados' main laboratory and study, but before the PCs can enter, they have to deal with **two zombie guards** who stand out of view in a pair of alcoves flanking the door. When anyone who hasn't been ritually marked as a Seeker nears the door, the zombies will emerge and attack. It shouldn't be hard for the PCs to defeat them—their purpose is to give Garados a moment of warning to prepare since he cast an alarm spell upon the zombies that will trigger when they move. A magical raven will suddenly appear and rush through the crack beneath the door in a burst of magic to warn him. Even though it might take more than one round to dispatch the zombie guards, the escalation die should reset when the PCs enter into the lab. The zombies have nothing of value.

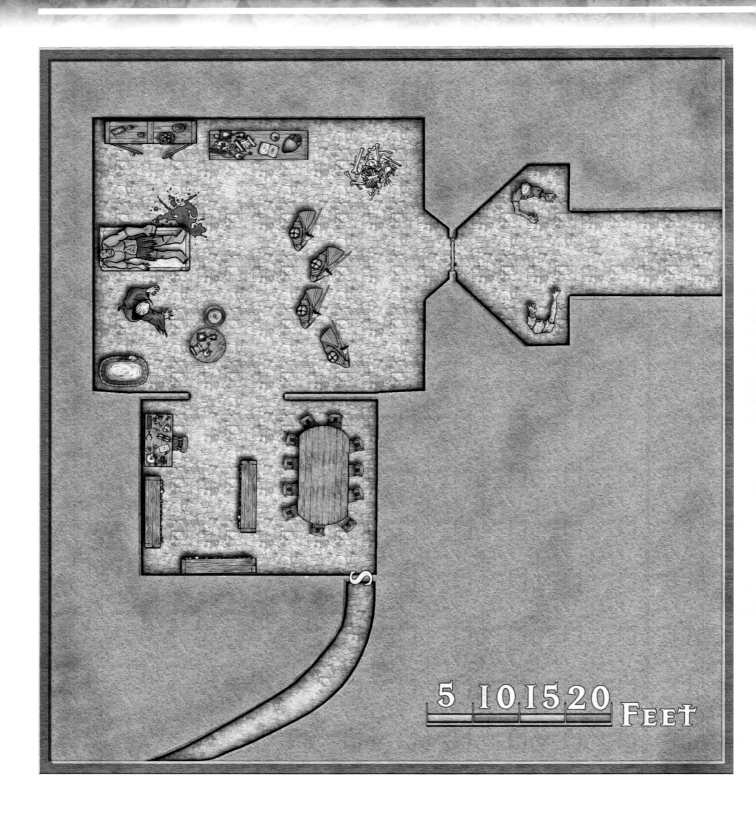

ZOMBIE GUARD

"Mwauurgh . . ."

0 level troop [UNDEAD]
Initiative: +0
Vulnerability: holy

Rotting fistslam +5 vs. AC—4 damage
　Natural 16+: The target is dazed, and the zombie takes 1d4 damage.

Headshot: A critical hit against a zombie guard drops it to 0 hp.

AC	14	
PD	12	**HP 16**
MD	9	

FACING GARADOS

Beyond the door is a two-part chamber that serves as a laboratory and study for Garados, and a meeting place for the Seekers. Garados will be waiting for the PCs in the lab, standing next to a stone table upon which rests his latest creation, a flesh golem. Unfortunately, the PCs disturbed his work before he could fully finish the golem, so it's not at full strength. In addition, Garados has animated a few skeletal warriors to keep foes off him. The following description assumes the PCs have encountered Garados previously at his shop. See the map opposite for a layout of the laboratory and study.

Read to the players: *The door opens to reveal a large rectangular chamber brightly illuminated by magic Lamplighter lanterns. A wide archway connects the room to another chamber to the left, which contains a large oval table and chairs, bookshelves, and smaller tables laden with apparatus, glass containers full of colorful liquids, and other arcane-looking tools. Standing directly in front of you are four skeletal figures with longswords held ready. Behind them at the back of the room is a tall, balding human in robes holding a staff and standing next to a large stone table—Garados! Lying on the table next to him is a huge humanoid figure.*

Garados frowns at you and says, "Your interference needs to end. So now I will let you see what it has all been about. Rise creature, and attack these living fools. I command it!" You see a monstrosity made from the flesh of many men push itself from the table, where it towers over everyone. One of its arms is shrunken and not fully formed. It looks at you with a single dead eye and raises a very large fist on its other well-muscled arm.

Tactics: The **four skeletal warriors** are arrayed across the width of the room and will hold their ground to intercept anyone trying to reach Garados/Kos (only one will move to intercept a PC doing so); on their first turn, they will then engage the PCs but use *mobile blocker* to defend Garados. The **incomplete flesh golem** will lumber toward the nearest PC and attack. It has limited intelligence and will attack whoever Garados/Kos commands it to attack, or whoever last made a melee attack against it or is nearest to it otherwise. If the PCs were forced to find the Seekers' Lair without Laredes help, Garados will also have **two zombie guards**, like those outside the door, standing on either side of the entrance in the laboratory.

Garados also has another surprise up his sleeve. Although he is a powerful wizard (see stats at the end of the adventure), he is overcautious in battle rather than arrogant in assuming victory. On his first turn before anyone else acts, he will use his familiar's *doppelganger* ability. As a standard action, he will turn invisible at the same moment that Kos, the homunculus familiar hiding in his robes, surrounds itself in an illusion resembling Garados. Unless a PC has some way of seeing such magical trickery, the switch will go unnoticed.

Garados will then move into the study and enter a secret door out of view of the main lab. He can look through Kos' eyes, speak through his mouth, and will watch the battle and try to learn about his adversaries as he escapes through the secret tunnel that connects to the Docks. Kos' true form as a homunculus resembles a small skeletal monkey-like humanoid—it was a special gift from the Lich King. Garados can also channel a limited amount of spell energy through Kos. **Kos as Garados** will attack the PCs beginning on the second round of combat. When reduced to 12 hp or less, Kos will attempt to flee out the main door and escape, dropping the illusion.

This is a double-strength battle, but if the PCs have taken enough incremental advances, it might not be as difficult for them. To make things more harrowing, you could add a level to the golem (+1 to attacks; +3 to each attack's damage; +20 hp). Alternately, if the battle feels too tough for the PCs, you could have the golem go into a rage once it's staggered: at that point it will attack a random creature each turn, allies included.

Also, if you want to have some fun, there should be a number of components and items on the lab tables that are explosive, acidic, poisonous, etc. if the PCs want to try to hurl something as a basic ranged attack. On a hit, the item deals 2d8 damage of the following type: 1. fire; 2. acid; 3. poison; 4. negative energy. On a miss, the PC takes 1d8 damage of that type (the beaker breaks in hand, etc.). There are 1d6 such items available, but all will become inert after a few minutes.

If there are only 4 PCs, remove 1 skeletal warrior and drop the golem's hit points by 20. If there are 6 PCs, add a skeletal warrior and increase the golem's stats by a level (as above). **Roll initiative!**

Skeletal Warrior

Scrape. Clang. Rattle.

1ˢᵗ level blocker [UNDEAD]
Initiative: +6
Vulnerability: holy

Longsword +5 vs. AC—5 damage

Mobile blocker: Once per round when an enemy tries to move behind this creature, the skeletal warrior can pop free from one enemy and move to intercept the moving enemy as a free action.

Resist weapons 16+: When a weapon attack targets this creature, the attacker must roll a natural 16+ on the attack roll or it only deals half damage.

AC	17	
PD	15	**HP 22**
MD	11	

Kos As Garados (Familiar)

"Heh, heh, heh."

3ʳᵈ level caster [CONSTRUCT]
Initiative: Kos and Garados go first each round

R: Magic missile (one enemy, no attack roll)—8 force damage

C: Chilling vapors +8 vs. PD (1d2 nearby enemies)—6 negative energy damage
Natural 16+: The target is dazed (save ends).
Limited use: 2/battle.

Doppelganger: Once per battle as a standard action, Kos's master can become invisible as Kos takes on its master's illusionary form. Kos can maintain the illusion each round at the start of its turn with a quick action. The illusion lasts until the end of the battle. Seeing through the illusion (if someone suggests there is one) requires a DC 20 Intelligence check (with magical backgrounds helping).

Illusory opponent: Because Kos as Garados is projecting an illusion of Garados and is actually quite small, each attack against AC or PD that hits him has a 25% chance of missing instead (miss damage applies) as it seems to pass through the wizard. Perceptive enemies who miss with an attack this way can try to detect the illusion for what it is with a DC 20 Wisdom check.

Tiny, quick construct: Kos gains a +5 bonus to disengage checks and a +5 bonus to all defenses against opportunity attacks. It also moves in leaping bounds that quickly outdistance normal humanoid movement once on the run (but can't maintain the illusion while doing so).

AC	18	
PD	14	**HP 40**
MD	16	

Incomplete Flesh Golem

"Graaaaaar!"

Large 3ʳᵈ level blocker [CONSTRUCT]
Initiative: +4

Massive fist +8 vs. AC—16 damage
Natural even hit: The golem can make a *smaller decaying fist* attack as a free action.
Natural odd hit: The target is dazed until the end of its next turn.
Miss: 4 damage.

[Special trigger] **Smaller decaying fist +6 vs. AC**—5 damage

C: Necrotic retch +6 vs. PD (1d2 nearby enemies)—11 negative energy damage, and the target is weakened until the end of the golem's next turn

Incomplete construct: When the golem crits with a melee attack, it also tears off a small piece of the target's flesh and presses it to its unformed arm, binding the new flesh. When it does this, it heals 2d6 hit points and gains a +2 bonus to attack and damage with *smaller decaying fist* (cumulative).

Energy magnet: Whenever a spell that causes cold, fire, force, or lightning targets one of the flesh golem's nearby allies, the flesh golem has a 50% chance of becoming the main target instead. Therefore, spells that affect groups would spread out from the flesh golem. Each time the golem takes negative energy damage, it heals 10 hp.

Weakness of the flesh: Unlike other golems, flesh golems are not immune to effects. Being constructed from the flesh of many, sometimes bloodily stitched together in the heat of battle, allows the golems to be affected by the fears and madness of mortals.

AC	18	
PD	16	**HP 80**
MD	14	

Loot: Searching the area reveals two more humanoid bodies with surgically removed organs and muscles lying in tubs along the back wall. Some of the magical equipment in the lab is rare and valuable, and would bring in 500 gp to the right buyer (like a wizard). The bookshelves contain tomes on anatomy, rituals for creating undead and constructs, and other dark topics. They are the sort of books the Archmage's people would want to confiscate and lock away, but on the black market they could be worth another 200 gp (100 gp reward from the Archmage's people).

There are also a handful of magic items on one of the workbenches that Garados was using to build the construct, including two **Potions of Healing** (adv), a **+1 Rune**, and a **Potion of Negative Energy Resistance**. In addition, there's a **Manual of Enlightened Flesh** that Garados was using to help him with the golem; it has a lot of notes in the margins about how the ideas in the book might apply to reanimated flesh.

The study holds a large table for the Seekers to meet, and various mundane items including a store of water, wine, and food. The secret door will be easy to find with a basic search.

AFTERMATH

Although Garados most likely escaped, and possibly his familiar Kos as well, there's enough evidence in the laboratory and study to implicate him as servant of the Lich King, as well as to identify another handful of Seekers of the Lost in town (though not all of them). By the time the PCs try to pick up Garados' trail, he'll be long gone, having immediately left town (most likely by ship) once he realized his secrets would be revealed. If the PCs go to the Silver Shields or Mage Council, they will be thanked and possibly rewarded (if you want to hand out another magic item and/or 500 gp, especially if the PCs didn't think to gather the lab equipment). The Silver Shields will round up the implicated Seekers and consider the matter closed. Garados, however, will continue his dark work for the Lich King in another location now that Eldolan is difficult for him.

With the job of discovering who was behind the zombie attack completed, the group is free to pursue other opportunities in Eldolan. The Silver Shields are still dealing with problems such as the imp causing trouble in the Docks district, or they might now be trying to corral the ochre jelly after the Eldritch Masters lost some students to the thing while trying to track it. Or if it fits your story better to take the PCs to a new location, perhaps the contact who put them on this job asks them to track down Garados and make him answer for his crimes. The PCs get sidetracked while following the trail, but eventually (around 3rd level) catch up with him as he is setting up a new network and will have a chance to make him answer for his crimes.

Another option would be to have new servants of the Lich King arise in Eldolan. The One-eyed Lord is unhappy with Garados botching the display of terror (pumpkinhead indeed) and someone truly terrifying, perhaps an intelligent undead monster, shows the town what fear really is.

Whatever the PCs decide to do next, they'll be better at it. Reward them with 2nd level if you haven't already!

NPC STATS

Here are stats for Garados and other NPCs the heroes might face at some point during the adventure.

GARADOS

Although it's unlikely the heroes will face Garados directly since he'll use his trick with Kos, here are stats for the wizard in case the PCs start something. Garados will generally try to flee if this happens, however, unless alone, he's probably more than a match for the PCs.

GARADOS, SEEKER OF THE LOST

"I'll be able to put your parts to many uses."

5ᵗʰ level caster [HUMANOID]
Initiative: +9

Darkness-infused dagger +9 vs. AC—10 damage, and 3 negative energy damage

R: Magic missile (up to two enemies, no attack roll) —8 force damage

R: Draining forcebolt +10 vs. PD (up to 2 nearby enemies in a group)—10 force and negative energy damage, and the target takes a –2 penalty to its next attack roll this battle
Natural 18+: The target is weakened until the end of its next turn, and Garados heals 2d8 hit points.

C: Grave mist +10 vs. PD (each nearby enemy)—8 negative energy damage
Natural even hit: The target is weakened (save ends).
Limited use: 1/battle.

Wizard's escape: Twice per battle as a move action, Garados can teleport anywhere nearby that he can see.

Lich King's loyal servant: The first time Garados would drop to 0 hp, each nearby enemy takes 5 negative energy damage and Garados heals an equal amount. (Add the healing to 0 hp; this is a free action that occurs before he would be slain.)

AC	20	
PD	15	HP 65
MD	21	

SILVER SHIELDS

Use these stats for the town guards if the PCs get caught performing an illegal activity, get framed by the Seekers for something, or as needed based on the story.

SILVER SHIELD SERGEANT

"What's going on here? Hands off those weapons!"

3ʳᵈ level leader [HUMANOID]
Initiative: +6

Short sword +8 vs. AC—8 damage
Natural even hit: The sergeant can make a *shield bash* attack as a free action.

[Special trigger] Shield bash (one engaged enemy)—4 damage, and the target is dazed (easy save ends, 6+).

Unit tactics: Roll a normal save at the start of each of the Silver Shield sergeant's turns. On a success, 1d2 of the sergeant's nearby allies can move or make a basic melee attack as a free action that turn as the sergeant yells out orders to them.

AC	20	
PD	17	HP 45
MD	14	

SILVER SHIELD WATCHER

"What's your business here?"

2ⁿᵈ level mook [HUMANOID]
Initiative: +5

Spear +7 vs. AC—5 damage

R: Light crossbow—4 damage

Pile on: When one or more watcher allies are engaged with its target, the watcher's melee attacks against that that target also daze it (save ends) with natural attack rolls of 18+.

Knows how to deal with wizards: The watcher gains a +2 bonus to all defenses against spell attacks or effects.

AC	18	
PD	15	HP 8 (mook)
MD	11	

Mook: Kill one silver shield watcher mook for every 8 damage you deal to the mob.

WIZARD SCHOOLS

All School wizards have the following ability, which they can use up three times each day as a standard action. The students use these tricks on rival school members and the general public.

Dirty cantrip trick: The wizard creates some minor magical effect that does not cause direct harm, but can cause trouble. For example, creating a bad stench somewhere nearby, making bodily noises or muffled sounds seem to come from a nearby creature, knocking over a stack of apples or causing a bucket of slops to spill over across someone's feet from a distance, making someone or their clothing appear strangely colored, etc.

ELDRITCH MASTERS PUPIL

"You're not smart enough to even understand how powerful I truly am!"

1st level mook [HUMANOID]
Initiative: +4

Short dagger +5 vs. AC—3 damage

R: Charging jolt +6 vs. PD—4 lightning damage
> *Natural 16+:* The pupil can make a second (but not a third) *charging jolt* attack against a different target as a free action.

Sizzling flames: Once per battle as a quick action, an eldritch masters pupil can pop free from all enemies as it creates a fan of flames around it. The flames do no real damage, though they could be used to light a flammable non-magical object.

AC	16	
PD	12	HP 6 (mook)
MD	15	

Mook: Kill one eldritch master pupil mook for every 6 damage you deal to the mob.

ELDRITCH MASTERS INSTRUCTOR

"You'll pay dearly for challenging the Eldritch Masters!"

2nd level caster [HUMANOID]
Initiative: +5

Ironwood cane +6 vs. AC—5 damage

R: Acid jet +7 vs. PD (up to 2 enemies in a group)—5 damage
> *Natural 16+:* The target takes 5 ongoing acid damage (save ends).

C: Forceful blowback +6 vs. PD (each enemy engaged with the instructor)—3 force damage, and the target pops free from the instructor
> *Quick use:* This power only requires a quick action (once per round) instead of a standard action when the escalation die is even.

Enhanced energy aura: As a standard action, the instructor can intone a spell of energy enhancement as it comments on proper form and casting. Each nearby eldritch master ally gains a +2 bonus to damage with spells until the start of its next turn.

AC	18	
PD	12	HP 34
MD	16	

MITHRIL PUPIL

"We are Mithril."

1st level mook [HUMANOID]
Initiative: +4

Weighted extendable rod +6 vs. AC—4 damage

R: Freezing bolt +6 vs. PD—4 cold damage

C: Elemental spray +5 vs. PD (1d3 nearby enemies)—2 damage of the following type of the GM's choice: cold, fire, acid, poison
> *Natural 16+:* The pupil draws upon an arcane component or slightly enchanted item in its possession (ring, pin, smooth stone, charcoal bit, iron bar, etc.) and transfers more energy to the spell. The target takes 3 extra damage of that type.

AC	16	
PD	13	HP 6 (mook)
MD	14	

Mook: Kill one mithril pupil mook for every 6 damage you deal to the mob.

MITHRIL INSTRUCTOR

"I can command the very elements of nature to do my bidding. You should run."

2nd level caster [HUMANOID]
Initiative: +5

Improvised artificing tool +6 vs. AC—6 damage

R: Streaking ball of flame +7 vs. PD—7 fire damage
> *Natural 16+:* The instructor can make a second (but not a third) *streaking ball of flame* attack as a free action.

C: Mithril's steel balls +7 vs. PD (1d2 nearby enemies in a group)—3 force damage
> *Natural even roll:* The target must roll a saving throw. On a failure, the target loses its next move action as it's blown into the air and off its feet.

AC	17	
PD	13	HP 36
MD	15	

ARCANISTS OF THE HIDDEN VEIL PUPIL

"You know nothing of TRUE power."

1st level mook [HUMANOID]
Initiative: +4

Razor-knuckle gloves +5 vs. AC—3 damage

R: Invisible stinging bites +6 vs. MD—3 damage, and 1 ongoing damage

C: Misdirecting shadows +5 vs. PD (each enemy engaged with the pupil)—The target takes a −2 penalty to attack the pupil until the end of its next turn due to partial blindness
> *Natural 16+:* The target also takes a −2 penalty to all defenses until the end of the pupil's next turn.

AC	16	
PD	10	HP 7 (mook)
MD	16	

Mook: Kill one hidden veil pupil mook for every 7 damage you deal to the mob.

ARCANISTS OF THE HIDDEN VEIL INSTRUCTOR

"You are wrong. Only we perceive the true reality."

2ⁿᵈ level caster [HUMANOID]
Initiative: +5

Hidden bully stick +6 vs. AC—5 damage

R: Force bolt (no attack roll)—3 damage

R: Phantasmal shadow monster +7 vs. MD—5 psychic damage, and 2 ongoing psychic damage
Natural odd hit: The target also takes a −2 penalty to attack rolls until it saves against the ongoing damage.

Shadow duplicates: Twice per battle, when a non-critical attack hits the instructor, it can roll an easy save (6+). On a success, the attack is a miss instead as a shadowy duplicate absorbs the attack while the instructor moves away.

AC	17	
PD	14	HP 36
MD	14	

OTHER PROBLEMS IN ELDOLAN

Use these stats if the PCs get involved with any of the other problems occurring in Eldolan, including the ochre jelly and rats, the imp and sailors in the Docks, or the warriors of the Crusader and Great Gold Wyrm. Some are straight out of the core rules.

OCHRE JELLY

"Is it just me, or did you see that puddle suddenly move?"

Large 3ʳᵈ level wrecker [OOZE]
Initiative: +2

C: Acid-drenched pseudopod +8 vs. PD (1d4 attacks, each against a different nearby enemy)—6 acid damage
Natural even hit or miss: 3 ongoing acid damage.

Splitter: The first time an ochre jelly takes 20 or more damage from a single attack, it splits into two normal-size ochre jellies, each with half the original's current hit points plus 2d6 hp for good luck. Treat the new jellies as undamaged jellies at their new hit point totals, but they don't have the *splitter* ability. (Maybe they get back together if they survive the fight. Maybe they don't.)

AC	18	
PD	17	HP 90
MD	16	

DIRE RAT

The biggest ones can rip your throat out quicker than you can scream.

1ˢᵗ level mook [BEAST]
Initiative: +2

Infected bite +5 vs. AC—4 ongoing damage

Carnage: The dire animal's attacks that miss deal damage equal to its level. When staggered, its missed attacks deal damage equal to double its level.

Squealing pack attack: This creature gains a +1 attack bonus for each other dire rat engaged with the target it's attacking.

AC	15	
PD	15	HP 6 (mook)
MD	10	

Mook: Kill one dire rat mook for every 6 damage you deal to the mob.

RAT SWARM

Pray you never hear the sound of hundreds of sharp tiny claws scrabbling toward you.

2ⁿᵈ level spoiler [BEAST]
Initiative: +4

C: Swarming bites +7 vs. PD (1d3 nearby enemies)—3 damage, and after the attack, the rat swarm engages one of the targets
Natural even hit: The target is hampered until the end of its next turn. It can end the effect by attacking the swarm, or if the swarm drops to 0 hp.

No opportunities: The rat swarm can't make opportunity attacks, and enemies can't make opportunity attacks against it.

Swarming resistance: Each turn, the rat swarm gains *resist damage 16+* to all damage from attacks by enemies that the swarm did NOT attack that turn.

AC	18	
PD	16	HP 39
MD	12	

COZORTL THE IMP

A few whispered words in the right ears can turn greed and lust to something worse.

3rd level spoiler [DEMON]
Initiative: +8

Festering claws +7 vs. AC—3 damage, and 5 ongoing damage

R: Blight jet +7 vs. PD—7 damage, and the target is dazed (save ends)
   First natural 16+ each turn: The imp can choose one: the target is weakened instead of dazed; OR the imp can make a *blight jet* attack against a different target as a free action.

Curse aura: Whenever a creature attacks the imp and rolls a natural 1–5, that creature takes 1d10 psychic damage.

Flight: Imps are hard to pin down because they fly. Not that fast or well, but you don't have to fly well to fly better than humans and elves.

AC	20	
PD	13	HP 40
MD	16	

IMP-INFLUENCED SAILORS

"Capt'n says we'll all be rich if we just take care of you."

1st level troop [HUMANOID]
Initiative: +3

Cutlass or club +6 vs. AC—5 damage

R: Hooked net +5 vs. PD—2 damage, and the target is stuck (save ends)
   Limited use: 1/battle, for every two sailors.

Terrain familiarity: When the sailors are fighting in familiar terrain, such as on their ship, or on a pier or in a tavern near where their ship is located, they gain a +1 bonus to attack, AC, and PD.

AC	16	
PD	14	HP 25
MD	12	

BLACKJACK, IMP-INFLUENCED CAPTAIN

"What are you looking at, drylander?"

Double-strength 2nd level wrecker [HUMANOID]
Initiative: +5

Cutlass and stiletto +7 vs. AC (2 attacks)—8 damage
   Natural odd hit: The target is dazed (−4 attack) until the end of its next turn as Blackjack pulls off a tricky or dirty attack.
   Miss: 2 damage.

R: Throwing knife +6 vs. AC—9 damage

Haze of greed and lust: Thanks to the imp's foul whisperings, Blackjack feels and acts invulnerable to the threats of enemies. At the start of each of his turns, he gains temporary hit points equal to twice the escalation die. If he is snapped out of this mindset somehow (DC 20 check), this effect is canceled and decrease his MD by 2.

AC	18	
PD	15	HP 65
MD	14	

SWORD OF THE GREAT GOLD WYRM

"Demons must be slain, not controlled!"

2nd level troop [HUMANOID]
Initiative: +4

Longsword +7 vs. AC—6 damage
   Natural 16+: The sword can make a *shield bash* attack as a free action.

[Special trigger] **Shield bash +6 vs. AC**—3 damage, and the target must roll an easy save (6+) or it's dazed until the end of its next turn

Devoted to the Great Gold Wyrm: A character with a positive or conflicted relationship with the Great Gold Wyrm gains a +4 bonus to checks when dealing with the sword. A character with a negative relationship with the Wyrm, or a positive or conflicted relationship with the Crusader takes a −4 penalty to checks when dealing with the sword.

AC	19	
PD	16	HP 35
MD	12	

CRUSADER STRIKE-TEAM SOLDIER

"If it weren't for us, you'd be staked out in the Abyss."

1st level troop [HUMANOID]
Initiative: +3

Sword, mace, or spear +7 vs. AC—6 damage
   Miss: 2 damage.

R: Javelin +6 vs. AC—5 damage
   Limited use: 3/battle.

Devoted to the Crusader: A character with a positive or conflicted relationship with the Crusader gains a +4 bonus to checks when dealing with the strike-team soldier. A character with a negative relationship with the Crusader, or a positive or conflicted relationship with the Great Gold Wyrm takes a −4 penalty to checks when dealing with the strike-team soldier.

AC	15	
PD	13	HP 24
MD	13	

DOCKS DISTRICT SHADY PATRONS

If the PCs start a fight they shouldn't, they could face the following shady patrons, one for each PC. Most likely, the battle will occur in the *Squirming Mermaid*, so set the scene as a dark tavern with a long bar, many tables and booths, a stairway up to a balcony, hanging chandeliers, or whatever else you think suits the location.

Each shady patron has a range of options on its melee attack to account for different skills of the roguish nature. It's also safe to say that if the PCs manage to defeat this group, they will gain the notice of the Prince's folk.

SHADY PATRON

"We don't like people asking too many questions."

3ʳᵈ level spoiler [HUMANOID]
Initiative: +7

Hidden knife +8 vs. AC—8 damage
Natural even hit: The shady patron chooses one: the target takes 5 extra damage; the shady patron pops free from the target; or the target takes a −2 attack penalty against the patron until the end of its next turn.

R: Hand crossbow/thrown knife +7 vs. AC—8 damage, and the shady patron pops free from one engaged enemy

Dwellers in the shadows: Before rolling initiative, roll one d6 for each shady patron in the battle. If you roll one or more 6s, one of the shady patrons has the following at-will sorcerous power.
R: Chaos bolt +7 vs. PD (one nearby or far away enemy)—12 damage
Natural 16+: The target is either dazed or vulnerable (save ends, GM's choice).

AC	19	
PD	17	**HP 45**
MD	13	

LAMPLIGHTER WIZARDS

If the PCs end up fighting their way into the Lanternwerks, or if you need a Lamplighter wizard leader who isn't a Seeker for another storyline, use Keloris, a female high elf Lamplighter Head Wizard.

KELORIS, LAMPLIGHTER HEAD WIZARD

"Who are you and what is going on here?"

3ʳᵈ level caster [HUMANOID]
Initiative: +6

Lampstaff +7 vs. AC—9 damage

R: Flame bolts +8 vs. PD (Up to two nearby enemies)—6 fire damage
Natural even hit: The target also takes 3 ongoing fire damage.
Miss: 3 ongoing fire damage.

C: Encroaching shadows +8 vs. MD (Each enemy engaged with Keloris)—The target can't see Keloris and has no line of sight to her until the end of its next turn as she is encased in shadows.

Trick of the light: When Keloris is staggered, as a free action she creates two shadowy duplicates of herself that stay close to her until the end of the battle. When an attack hits her, the attacker must roll a normal save. On a failure, the attack hits a shadowy duplicate instead. On a success, it hits her. When a duplicate is hit, it dissipates. After both duplicates dissipate, attackers no longer have to roll the save to hit her.

AC	18	
PD	13	**HP 41**
MD	18	

KEY NPCS/LOCATIONS

GENERAL NPCS

Arlissa Thent: human Lamplighter wizard; Lanternwerks administrator; Seeker agent

Cornelius: gnome Lamplighter wizard at Lanternwerks

Cornigar Ulson: ancient human wizard; lead instructor of the Mithril school

Garados Kessmir: head of Lamplighter's Guild; leads the Seekers of the Lost

Jarlin the Sly: gnome wizard and illusionist; lead instructor of the Arcanists of the Hidden Veil

Laredes the Sage: human wizard and sage; business partner to Garados at the Emporium

Mabs: halfling cutpurse who might be tailing the PCs

Nightshade: drow female assassin working for Samuel

Samuel: male human Seeker wizard/hit man

Sergeant Parelles: human Silver Shield guardsman responding to zombie attack

Sharissa Darkbolt: high elf wizard; lead instructor of the Eldritch Masters

LEAD 1 NPCS/COMMONS

Capper: human teenage Ratsmasher gangmember; well-spoken

Elsa Whiterose: runs the Mission of Lost Hope

Jagger Dunn: dwarf drunk/laborer; street contact

Jarsil Ralss: halfling cage dealer at Dreammaster's theater

Kalia the Waif: female half-elf street urchin (girl); street contact

Korack Stoneson: missing dwarf drunk turned into a zombie

Riley Threefinger: male halfling fence; street contact

Sigmund & Paulos: Seeker thugs working for Dreammaster

Tolvus Rhys: missing human street person turned into a zombie

Torsar Blacktooth, aka the Dreammaster: drug dealer

LEAD 2 NPCS/DOCKS

Aerto: half-elven (drow) fixer in Docks; Seeker agent; found at *Squirming Mermaid*

Jeskill: human Diabolist cultist

Jiggs: dirty, bedraggled, older gnome man; found at *Sailor's Respite*

Malice Sureshot: wiry halfling woman; found at *Wild Wave Inn* taproom

Michale Orlevy: male human scoundrel and bard; found at *Lusty Dolphin*

Scarlet Ylas: high elven woman; former pirate; owner of *Squirming Mermaid*

Talina Brighteyes: half-elven woman; found at *Westwind Tavern*

Travan Orcslayer: crusty, older male dwarf; found at *Dwarves Home Alehouse*

LEAD 3 NPCS/COMMONS/TEMPLES

Brother Thomas: cleric acolyte at Dead Vaults; escort to crypts

Koln: human friend of Rollo who died; turned into a zombie

Landon Smithson: Dead Vaults acolyte; Seeker agent

Odessa Rilantes: human woman, head cleric at Dead Vaults

Rollo the Thin: male halfling merchant in Hawker's Square

LEAD 4 NPCS/SADDLE

Grayson, aka Abrose Fuller: Seeker agent at Old Brewery; cart buyer

Jalen: assistant to Grayson, the brains behind "pumpkinhead"

Pazarius Rane: half-elf merchant/wagoner; sold cart to Grayson

Rumney Twosilvers: dwarf craftsman; witness of the attack

POSSIBLE MAGIC ITEMS IN THE ADVENTURE

Help from Icons

2 vials of divine tears of Halatir, patron saint of Eldolan. There are two ways to use this blessed water: apply it to a weapon or use it as a weapon.

- Applying it to a weapon (a standard action) makes attacks with that weapon deal holy damage. The effect lasts until the end of the battle.
- Making an attack using **holy water** is a standard action. **R: Dexterity or Wisdom + Level vs. PD (one nearby undead or demon enemy)**—1d6 holy damage per level.

2 Potions of Healing: +1d8 hp; 30 hp max

Potion of Negative Energy Resistance: 16+

+1 Rune

+1 Armor of Iron Will: AC bonus also applies to MD. *Quirk:* Prone to abstract speculation.

+1 [Weapon] of Protection (melee): Recharge 6+; when you make a basic attack with the weapon, gain a +4 bonus to all defenses until the end of your next turn. *Quirk:* Tremendous appetite for meat.

+1 Implement/Wand of the Mage's Invisible Aegis: Recharge 16+; Cast the wizard's shield spell at a level no higher than yours. *Quirk:* Hums tunelessly.

Lead 1/Dreammaster's Theater

Bearclaw Necklace: Recharge 11+; when you hit with a melee attack while you're staggered, gain 10 temporary hp. *Quirk:* Swaggers even when overmatched.

Lead 2/Cultist Summoning Cave

+1 Rune: +1 bonus to AC or to attack/damage, plus random effect

+1 Holy Relic of Destruction: +1 attack and damage with a divine spell/attack; *Recharge 11+;* when you hit an enemy with an attack that deals holy damage, deal 1d10 extra holy damage with that attack. *Quirk:* Believes the world will come to a fiery end . . . soon.

Lead 3/Aid from Odessa

2 Potions of Healing: +1d8 hp; 30 hp max

1 vial of divine tears of Halatir: see above

Charm of Negative Energy Resistance: one-use item, quick action to activate; gain *resist negative energy 16+* for one battle or five minutes.

Gained from Arlissa Thent

Potion of Fire Resistance: standard action, gain *resistance 16+* to fire attacks

Gloves of Mind Rot: Recharge 6+; when you hit with an arcane spell attack, deal +1d10 psychic damage to one target. *Quirk:* The texture of your skin seems wrong to everyone else, but you know it's all in their minds and often it that to them.

Gained from Garados' Laboratory

2 Potions of Healing (adv): +1d8 hp; 30 hp max

+1 Rune: +1 bonus to AC or to attack/damage, plus random effect

Potion of Negative Energy Resistance: standard action, gain *resistance 16+* to negative energy attacks

Manual of Enlightened Flesh: Gain a +1 bonus to all skill checks based on Strength, Constitution, or Dexterity. *Quirk:* Takes heightened satisfaction in their own physical prowess.